STORY

The Art of Learning From Your Past

JIM PIPER

Published by Freiling Agency, LLC.

P.O. Box 1264
Warrenton, VA 20188

www.FreilingAgency.com

HB ISBN: 979-8-9897784-8-5
eBook ISBN: 979-8-9897784-9-2

Printed in the United States of America

Dedication

My most important story can't be told without my family, so I've dedicated this work to them. Each and every one has been used by God to shape me and help me see the majestic gift of life. I especially mention my seven grandchildren, the next generation.

James William Piper, IV
Jaxson James Piper
Roxann Celeste Piper
Macy Grace Martinez
Major Gregory Martinez
Reagan Ann Piper
Maverick Grayson Martinez

Each of these souls have added invaluable meaning and significance to my life. Their presence inspires me to be better. To love deeper and reach higher. To each, I have assigned nicknames which are expressions of my affection. I can't imagine my life without them. I pray God's grace and blessings on each of them to overcome obstacles, to have faith believing they are loved, and to have courage to live out their days with purpose. To be chasers after God while leaving no small ripple upon this planet. To co-author with God their unique stories.

Contents

PART III
LEADERSHIP STORIES THAT SHAPE US

Introduction

According to Christian Scripture, your life is meaningful and significant. You have intrinsic value. It is also unique. Your life is a story made up of many stories. It is a mosaic, beautiful in the eyes of the discerning.

Your stories include a variety of people. Some you barely remember and others who made a unique impression on your soul. Some of these people belong to you by choice and others are inescapable. In a sense, the living narrative of your life is bigger than you.

Your story is not your own. It belongs in part to others. It belongs to God. It animates your existence and radiates beyond your physical boundaries. Your story is an eternal impression upon creation.

Over the last four decades, I have made it my business to notice and learn from stories. While working as a young business banker, my eyes were open to creativity, problem solving, wisdom, finance, and greed. As a pastor, I'm introduced to the personal struggles of the human condition causing me to dive deeper in search for truth beyond the platitudes of religion and positive thinking. As a coach and consultant, I have seen the power of faith-centric leaders in partnership with God. And as host of The Today Counts Show, a life and leadership podcast, all I do is learn!

WHAT THIS BOOK IS ABOUT

The purpose of this book is to encourage you. To remind you of your value and the importance of your stories. Past, present, and future. To inspire you to co-author your life's narrative alongside your creator and the people in your life. To allow reflection and application to shape your character and your leadership.

To do this, we will consider stories from childhood, stories where certain people have made significant impressions upon us, and the implications all of these can have on our development as people and leaders. The first section of this book looks back in time to appreciate the past—the good, bad, and ugly. To realize the things behind us are useful for the present and the future. This helps you understand, in part, who you are today. It allows you to evaluate and decide what is good or bad and what you will choose to do moving forward.

Who are the people in your story? The second section of this book will remind you how powerful relationships are to your life and story. Your role in them. What they have taught you. What they can teach you. How they can hurt you and how they can help you. This section should also help you see the power of your presence in the lives of others.

Why does it matter? Articulating your story and the impact others have had in your story exponentially improves your leadership. When you examine your story, appreciate and see it with new eyes, you become a better leader. You are more self-aware. You lead yourself more effectively. You relate to others more intentionally. And as a result, you become a better person and a better leader. When that happens, everyone benefits.

WHO THIS BOOK IS WRITTEN FOR

This book is for the believer. For those who believe their life counts. For those who believe or want to believe what is right, good, and helpful. It is for those who desire to live a positive, purposeful, and courageous life. For those who desire to be at peace within themselves. And it's for those who strive to align their attitudes and actions to their central beliefs. It's for those who desire to create a worldview founded on ancient wisdom, tempered by experience, and fueled with purpose.

This book is for the person who desires healthy and productive relationships. For those who want to be a blessing. For those who want to belong, to know and be known. For those who want to be an example for others. For those who are willing to take responsibility.

This book is for the leader. For the person who desires to steward their opportunities to better the lives of others. For the listener. The learner. For those who see themselves as a servant to those they lead. It's for the person who actually believes they can make a difference.

This book is not for the thin-skinned who are easily offended. Not for the one who cries foul at every experience of injustice. It's not for the thick-skulled who do not have an open mind. Not for the know-it-all. It is for the reasonable, the curious, the idealist, and the rational. It's for most of us but not all of us.

I've done my best to apply sound theology, logic, empathy, and experience to this work. I borrow many stories from my own life and the lives of others for illustrative purposes, many you will relate to and appreciate. It is my prayer and desire that you will be encouraged as you align your life, relationships, and leadership to what is true, causing all of Heaven to stand and take notice of your story.

PART I

CHILDHOOD STORIES
THAT SHAPE US

"God is big enough
to be small enough to care
about you."

—Jim Piper, Jr.

"

"There is no greater agony
than bearing an untold story
inside you."

—Maya Angelou

"

The Power of Your Story

I went to church camp on occasion. Some of my best memories come from around the campfire. There always seemed to be a good story teller who would take center stage and command the attention of us all. The characters within the story always resembled those gathered around the fire. Dark as dark can be with stars in the sky, the master storyteller swept us away into another place and time. Always filled with mystery and danger, they somehow ended in relief laced with a life-lesson and warning.

As I write this first chapter, we are only a few days away from my grandkids coming to visit. We will have the outdoor fireplace going, the smores roasting, and yes, a good story from grandpa. Stories are powerful. They are easier to remember than concepts, principles, or statistics. They engage the listener, evoke emotion, inspiration, and action. A well written story causes the reader to escape their current reality and come alive within the pages of the narrative. Stories persuade and teach. They have the power to pass down virtues and traditions.

All of life is a story. We watch stories called movies and shows. We watch and experience the stories of our children as they grow up. We are a living story. Every hour, every day, we are making stories, watching them, and living in them. Our stories are shaping us. Not just the experiences of our lives but the people within our stories. The witnesses. The friends and the foes. The heroes and villains. The betrayers and the beloved. All are the cast of characters in our story.

Your life is a series of stories. It is made up of decades and seasons. Hopes and dreams. Victories and defeats. Some hours feel like a year and some years fly by like an hour. And as I said in the introduction, your story is a mosaic. A masterpiece. Your story has power.

Every story has ups and downs. Significant points of highs and lows. Imagine watching a movie or reading a book without drama. Without loss or difficulty. Without courage or victory. It would be boring, unrealistic, and an absolute waste of time.

In the movies, the characters often make mistakes. Big ones! Some recover from them and some don't. We watch with great interest because we imagine being in the same situation. Why? Because we have. What makes a movie really good is when it mirrors reality. When it portrays the truth. When it identifies with our experiences. Especially when it inspires us to make a comeback. To fight back. To win.

We don't like stories that seem fake. That leaves out failures, disappointments, tragedies, and mistakes. We have a need to feel those. To identify with them. To acknowledge that they exist. That's why we love movies based upon true events. We need to know that we are not alone. Bad things happen to all of us yet we get through them while searching for reason, purpose, and hope for a new day.

You rewind your stories. You tell yourself about the good times but you prefer to forget the bad ones. You like to remember the victories but push back the losses. You embrace your moments of brilliance while beating yourself up for the mistakes. But to get power from your stories, you must squeeze out the good and the bad. The bad teaches you as much or perhaps even more than the good.

As you read this book, my prayer is that you will come to deeply appreciate your story. To embrace it. To reframe it and align it to truth by faith. Your story is being created through your partnership with God. Reflect upon the individual stories and seasons of your life. The good, bad, and ugly. In doing so, you will learn. You will digest acceptance, meaning, and wisdom. You will be able to see how God transforms any story into a masterpiece. Your story is a miracle in the making. If you're willing to see it.

"And what do you benefit if you gain the whole world but lose your own soul? Is anything worth more than your own soul?"

—Matthew 16:26, NLT

Give Me That Old-Time Religion

"Jimmy Boy, why are you being a bad guy to your parents?" These words walked right out of my mouth as I was caught off guard by my three-year-old grandson's behavior. I hadn't seen him in a while because he and his parents moved to Germany on assignment from the United States Air Force. The two of us had grown close because he and his mother lived with us while my son was in training. The last time I saw him, he was near perfect, so his behavior startled me.

My question got his attention. He looked me square in the eyes with a furrowed brow and said, "I'm not a bad guy! I'm a good guy!" I was shocked, relieved, and humored all at the same time. What he heard struck him in the heart. He heard his loving grandfather call him a bad guy. I certainly was accusing him of acting poorly but I had not reached a final verdict on the matter. Come to think of it. Is there a difference between acting like a bad guy and being a bad guy? Go back with me to the year 1968 when I was an eight-year-old boy.

My palms were sweaty and my face flushed. Maybe it was the room temperature or maybe it was the war raging within me. I accepted the pastor's invitation, stepped out from the pew and made my way to the church altar. There is where and when I was introduced to the Sinner's Prayer.

The Sinner's Prayer

Perhaps you've heard of the Sinner's Prayer. If you haven't, I'm confident you've heard of Billy Graham. The Billy Graham Evangelistic Association crafted their own version of this prayer and is widely used in one form or another within many Christian communities.

> Dear God, I know I'm a sinner, and ask for your forgiveness. I believe Jesus Christ is Your Son. I believe that He died for my sin and that you raised Him to life. I want to trust Him as my Savior and follow Him as Lord, from this day forward. Guide my life and help me to do your will. I pray this in the name of Jesus.

For the person raised in the church, the prayer may seem common-place or simple. However, that could not be farther from the truth. A closer look reveals the prayer is actually a profound out-of-this-world confession. Let's take a quick look at each major phrase along with the implications.

- *Dear God, I know I'm a sinner, and ask for your forgiveness.*

You acknowledge there is a God and He has established standards you have missed. You believe your life matters, that's why there is an accounting for it. You recognize your need and desire for forgiveness.

- *I believe Jesus Christ is Your Son.*

You believe Jesus is the way to God. You believe He is God the Son (notice the uppercase S in Son, linguistically illustrating deity). God has a son? Yes, but not in the way you are thinking. He is not the offspring of God. He is not less than God. There is too much to unpack here; so, for now, consider these points:

Jesus means "God saves, rescues, delivers."
Christ is a title: "Messiah", "Anointed One".

You might recall the name Immanuel, in various Christmas songs; it's another name for Jesus, which means, "God with us".

- *I believe that He died for my sin and that you raised Him to life.*

You know there are laws within God's design. Perhaps the most significant and commonly experienced is reaping and sowing. You tend to look negatively at it even though it was designed to provide great blessings and harvests. As a sinner, you will reap physical death. Your body will die. Your soul is also in grave danger. However, because of what Christ has done for you (born without sin, lived without sin, and became the acceptable agent who bore our sin), He precedes you in resurrection providing you the opportunity to follow Him into eternity with an upgraded, new, and incorruptible body. In other words, the dead will live again.

- *I want to trust Him as my Savior and follow Him as Lord, from this day forward.*

Because of what Christ has done, there is nothing left for you to do except to believe Him, to trust Him. You don't deserve it. You can't earn it. He is your Savior from the final death. He won't force Himself upon you. The only thing you can do now is trust Him and follow Him. Make Him the boss (Lord) of your life.

- *Guide my life and help me to do your will. I pray this in the name of Jesus.*

The Bible teaches you more about following Christ. It teaches you more about God. It teaches you how to listen and learn His ways. You want this. You end the prayer in the name of Jesus because He told us to ask God for whatever we need using His name. When you honor the name of Jesus, you are confessing Him to be the ruling authority of life, your life. God honors that.

It's a simple prayer with a profound result.

Three Times Frontward

Let me finish the story. Pastor McClellan's message was simple. "Somebody has to pay for your sin. Either you or Jesus. It's your choice." I'm skipping a lot of content but that was the bottom line. It was like jumping into a mountain stream in spring, startling yet refreshing.

Well, for me, that was an easy decision! I chose Jesus! Minutes later, my choice resulted in a face-to-face discussion with the pastor. I see him in my childhood mind as a taller man in a suit, tie, glasses, a big Bible, the whole nine yards. However, if you showed me a picture of him today, I'd probably see a stranger. Afterall, that was well over a half-century in the rearview mirror.

He asked me a number of break-the-ice questions. I'm sure I responded with the standard one syllable answers kids tend to offer. Yes, no, or the shaking of my head. I cannot remember his tone of voice but I was never intimidated or fearful being in his presence. Well, except for the baptism.

During our man-to-man encounter, he explained why people get baptized, encouraging me to do the same. Made sense to me until I found myself gowned next to him in the baptismal pool later that evening at "night church". In view of the congregation and my family, fear fell upon me.

Back at his office, he described what baptism looked like. He would stand next to me, immerse me frontwards (face first) in and out of the water, three times. The first dunking would be in the name of the Father, the second, in the name of the Son, and the third, in the name of the Holy Spirit. But there was one thing we did not cover. Should I try to hold my breath all the way through the sequence or sneak in a quick one between the dunkings?

Life Lesson: What's your story? How have you wrestled with the meaning of life? How have you dealt with the idea of a Supreme Being?

All adults have been shaped by their childhood environments and experiences, more than you think or want to believe. Whether positive childhood experiences (PCEs), or adverse childhood experiences (ACEs), each leave their significant marks upon our soul. This reality shapes what we believe. Does it make what we believe true? Of course not.

Some will need to work diligently to differentiate their childhood programming from what they really believe. Their inner child needs to grow up. For others, childhood is the advantage. Convictions established early only become stronger and more useful. Becoming a fully developed and healthy adult is hard work. Is this why the Hebrew Scriptures implore parents to be diligent in the raising of their children? Is raising their children toward faith a parent's greatest opportunity? Think about the opportunity to partner with God in the creation of the next generation. Is this how He designed it?

"Teach them [The ways of God] *to your children. Talk about them when you are at home and when you are on the road, when you are going to bed and when you are getting up."*

—Deuteronomy 11:19, NLT

"When I paid a visit to my past,
it unmasked the lies, revealed the
truths, and equipped me for
the days ahead."

—Jim Piper, Jr.

Confirmation or Deconstruction

As the years rolled by, now a young man, I wanted to find that almost forgotten church while introducing my wife to some of my history. When we arrived, the doors were unlocked. We walked through the entry and into the fellowship hall which also served as the pathway to the sanctuary. As we shuffled along at tortoise speed, memories fell upon me like the force of a waterfall I once stood under in beautiful Hawaii.

I was surprised by the vivid colors and details of my memories. I could hear the laughter and voices of young boys playing and competing during our Boys' Brigade gatherings. I could almost smell the feasts we would share around the church wide communion celebrations.

I could see familiar faces of the past. I saw Mr. Eastman, my Sunday School teacher, ceremoniously washing my feet as an act of humility and service, core values of the Brethren. Foot washing was a common practice for this faith community. One would place their feet in a tray of water while sitting on a chair. The other, kneeling with a towel in hand, would lightly splash water over the feet and then dry. Words of edification would often be expressed during the ritual. The participants would switch places and repeat.

As I stepped back into the present, we reverently entered the sanctuary. I was awed by its size and simplicity. It was so very small! Not how I remembered it. My eight-year-old mind saw it as a cathedral, complicated, supernatural, mostly for big words and big people. But as a young adult man then, I was struck with thoughts and feelings of gratitude for this place and the people who made it what it was for me. A nest where I was fed, loved, accepted, belonged, and at some point, set free.

I've never regretted my child-like faith and the years we spent at that little church and school. I certainly don't agree with everything I experienced there but I've never felt a need to deconstruct the foundations of my faith. In fact, my childhood has always been to my advantage. It laid for me a foundation of strength and stability in an unstable world. It protects me from foolishness and pride. It is an inner force difficult to describe yet very present.

After finishing my business degree, I went on to study and earn an advanced degree in theology. What did I experience there? What did I learn? I experienced some clarity and a fair share of unsolved mysteries. I learned how to think a little better, fitting together some of the lofty logic of theology while feeling the desperate needs of humanity. It was the combination of these two that helped me coin a phrase I still use today: ***God is big enough to be small enough to care about you***. Perhaps it's an oversimplification for some but it has certainly provided me with a sense of grace and freedom.

I've also met some amazing, bright, and sincere people in the halls of academia. But what have I learned best? What has stuck with me most? Confessions of faith are profound. They are the pathways to confirmation. To me, confirmation is an intentional and sometimes intense process of working out one's deeply held values and beliefs. The reward for such work is inner peace and confidence while still leaving room for uncertainty but never to the extent of despair.

There is certainly good and bad theology, good and not-so-good religious convictions. I suppose you can make a case for this and a case for that. What my childhood baptism, THREE TIMES FRONTWARD, taught me is that we become better people and better leaders as we approach every topic, opportunity, and season of life with a kid's curious mindset.

Young or old, God admires humility. He loves it when we acknowledge dependence on His grace, mercy, and power. Answers and solutions seem to flow to those who seek Him. So, if leaders choose to get small, they often become great because God loves transforming small into big!

THE POWER IN YOUR CONFESSION

Your life is a bit of a paradox. You can do with it what you want but if what you want is outside of God's design, you won't be successful. However, if you embrace the idea that God's way is the obvious and best choice, you will flourish. When your soul is aligned with God's design, good things happen. So, where do you start?

You begin by embracing your responsibility for making confessions. A confession is simply a belief animated in your daily life. People live what they believe without ever recognizing it. So, if you begin to speak what you believe or take notice of what you do, it just might cause you to rethink those ideas.

You have already made confessions about what you believe or don't believe by the way you live. But have you accepted the responsibility for doing so? Decisions follow confessions. Confessions are not always easy to make. You need information. You need verification. You need conviction. For me, the Sinner's Prayer was the confession that continues to reap good decisions.

Good decisions have lasting effects just as poor ones do. You can never be too young or too old to make life-changing decisions. Whether you are eight or eighty, you need to make a decision. Though I made my first significant confession at the age of eight, some of us are given the grace to make confessions of faith right at the final horn.

Recently, my wife's sister, Darlene, passed into eternity rather suddenly at the age of seventy due to heart failure. She did not live what most of us would call a life of piety. Far from it I'm afraid. While cleaning out her apartment, one of her sisters stumbled upon a handwritten note. It said:

Dear God, I want to thank you first for all of the blessings you have given me. I ask on bended knees, forgiveness for my sins. My life is yours. I surrender my all to you. Make me white as snow. Refresh my mind and soul. Heal me from my pain and sufferings. I ask that you cover my family and friends with blessings and protection. I love you and want you in my life. Amen, my Lord Jesus.

There is a line in a song our church sings. It says, "If you're not dead, He's not done." We do not know when Darlene wrote this confession but we are confident it was not long before her physical heart stopped. We are grateful for God's mysterious ways and mercy even in the final hours.

The confession I made many years ago, set a course of confirmation or should I say, confirmations, for the rest of my life. It became foundational for everything that followed. You might be tempted to believe an eight year old's decision is not very important because of the psychological development and station at that point in one's life. While it's certainly true that many decisions in our youth are confined to the short term, it's also true that a simple decision at one point in life can grow and develop into a deep and sophisticated conviction. That's because a person's cognitive agency involves three significant components: intellect, emotion, and will. More on that in the next chapter.

Life Lesson: If your faith story sprung into life as a child or you're one of the minority who came to faith in your adult years, you have a new mission in life. Scripture says, you have been GIVEN the ministry of reconciliation. That means you have become an ambassador of heaven. Your life's story is about becoming a blessing to others! If you have not, let me encourage you to begin speaking your confessions. Watch what happens. Go farther, do the hard work to write your confessions. They will become the foundation for your decisions. And your decisions will change the course of your life.

"And God has given us this task of reconciling people to him… So we are Christ's ambassadors; God is making his appeal through us."

—2 Corinthians 5:18-20, NLT

"The consequences of our actions
are always waiting for us
in the future."

—Jim Piper, Jr.

We're Not Kids Anymore

I'm well into my sixties as I write this yet I can recount without labor about half a dozen decisions from my childhood that have the power to evoke emotions of guilt and shame. Half of these "decisions" were not isolated acts, they were patterns of behaviors. Let me run to my defense, to yours, and to all children on this planet. It takes time for kids to realize they have the power to think about the kind of person they want to be and make decisions to that end before they encounter various temptations. Until then, our failures only reveal our ignorance.

It's true for me and it's true for you. What I want today can distract me from what I want tomorrow. Making decisions rooted deeper in conviction requires the rational side of our being to be challenged. It has to be tested. It has to make sense to some degree of satisfaction. For something to be convincing does not mean you are left without any doubts or unanswered questions. It simply means, you are convinced that your conclusion is the best and most logical answer within a realm of lesser possibilities. The more our rationale overcomes various and seasonal attacks on our conviction, the more secure and confident we become.

Sometimes we make decisions from our emotional self, only later to discover the error of the decision.

These kinds of choices often disappoint. Liken your emotions to your youngest brother. He finds himself in a bad situation calling out to his big brother, the Rational, to come rescue him. And that he does with the assistance and power of the other brother, Will, or as some call him, Will Power. While we sometimes make fun of our emotions, let's remember that he is a very important part of our cognitive agency. Simply put, something can make logical sense but if you don't love it, you don't love it. You will probably decide against the things that don't draw out your affections. You won't be able to engage your will.

Once you are convinced of a matter and your affections embrace it, your will, the ability to act with determination, steps up and steps in to execute. The human will is a God-given and mysterious power. It's another example of God's presence in your life. What amazes me most about the will is its ability to rise up and face the difficult and seemingly impossible challenges of life, even when your rational self knows the odds are not in your favor. If there is a chance, no matter how slight, and the affections are strong, the fight to win begins. For these reasons we learn that some decisions are made in a miracle moment while others may be years or decades in the making.

Make no mistake. The ability to choose, to decide, to act, is a power bestowed on you. When you make decisions in a morally responsible way, we call it courage. Thomas Paine, one of America's Founding Fathers, may have said it best:

> *"I love the man that can smile in trouble, that can gather strength from distress, and grow brave by reflection. 'Tis the business of little minds to shrink; but he whose heart is firm, and whose conscience approves his conduct, will pursue his principles unto death."*

It's the principles and the convictions behind our decisions that determine their longevity. The decision of an eight-year-old may seem like a mere acorn to some but in time it grows into an oak of whose branches grandchildren can swing. If a child can make a significant decision and it is nurtured for growth, what is a fully capable adult with countless resources able to do?

As an adult, you've seen plenty of tragedy in this world. And in some cases, it seems society has lost its collective mind. What other evidence do you need to make counter-cultural, life-changing decisions today? Before it's too late.

LIFE-GIVING DECISIONS

In 2007, I decided to start Lead Today, a non-profit organization dedicated to serving and shaping leaders of character. My target audience is anyone who considers themselves a learner and a leader. I know plenty of so-called leaders but to find one who is also an intentional learner, well, that is a joy! My emphasis in the name Lead Today is on the word "Today". The decisions we make today affect our tomorrow and the day after that and the day after that.

In 2022, I started The Today Counts Show & podcast. My audio engineer, Mike Hines, wrote a script for me describing the purpose of our podcast and the idea behind the name. And wouldn't you know, he penned the words, *Today Counts because it impacts and influences your tomorrows and the day after that and the day after that.*

Today does count. You can make a good decision today that has the potential to change your life exponentially while also impacting the lives of those you love and lead. When we become better people and better leaders, everyone benefits. What decisions for good have you been ignoring? What tough decisions do you need to make? I believe the most important decision a person can make has to do with their relationship with God. Without God, life is a deadend. With God at the center, life takes on a whole new purpose.

Many find themselves in a place where growing is no longer a priority and certainly not a habit. For some, listening to insightful podcasts, reading worthy material, or sitting under religious studies, have fallen to the wayside. Theirs is a life-style of skimming. Nothing is deep. Everything is busy and superficial. Learning or being influenced is reduced to watching and listening to social media soundbytes. "Busy" has become the thief stealing important opportunities to make wise and life-changing decisions.

Let's choose differently. Before we step into the next chapters, consider the following questions. They are the "go to" questions I ask many of the leaders I serve. Read them, think about them, and answer them with honesty and courage.

- *What things (habits, employment, attitudes, relationships) are you doing now and believe you should continue to do?* This is the process of identifying the things of excellence that need to be protected.
- *What things will you stop doing?* These might be unhelpful thoughts you ponder. They may be addictions to conquer. They might even be good things but they take time away from the most important things.
- *What things will you start doing?* Sometimes, the best way to remove unhealthy activities is to replace them with healthy ones.

Life Lesson: I've learned that decisions are habit forming. Good decisions give birth to more good decisions. Bad decisions give birth to more bad decisions. Whichever road you take, that road becomes the one easier to stay on and more difficult to leave, depending upon your perspective.

There's not much you can do about the decisions you made in the past. If they were good, you are still reaping the benefits. If they were bad, you might be feeling the effects even today. If you follow through on your answers to the questions above, you've taken an important step writing the next chapter of your life. The longer term you think, the better decisions you will make. Your decisions live much longer than you realize. Choose wisely.

"Tolerance is the virtue of the man
without convictions."

—Gilbert K. Chesterton

Environments That Shape Convictions

People with strong convictions animate them in their daily behaviors. One's closely held values cannot be contained in theory. If they are still forming inside the egg of theory, they have not yet been hatched. But once the shell is cracked and the conviction walks out, we can see what has developed.

Our childhood is a most powerful incubator for convictions. Sometimes they are stated in a negative or defensive posture to guard from harmful experiences of the past. For example, while we all advocate for the safety of our children, those who have first hand experience with childhood abuse have a heightened awareness. In other words, one might use a phrase like "Safe Environments," while another will say, "Protect the Children!" Both are saying the same thing but one has been personally impacted by the horror of a dark reality. While each is given innate and unchanging temperaments, we are significantly shaped and even modified by the conditioning of our childhood.

BOYS' BRIGADE

"So God created man in His own image; in the image of God He created him; male and female He created them."   —Genesis 1:27

Fire trucks pulled up onto the church parking lot because someone reported a fire. Actually, there were dozens of fires but they were really small. We boys were frying burgers on mini self-made camp stoves. We learned how to transform large and empty coffee cans into portable stoves, and fry hamburgers. It was a blast! Together, we created a cloud of good smelling smoke for all the neighbors to enjoy, or so we thought.

I don't remember if any of the firemen had the opportunity to taste our wonderful creations, but if they did, I'm sure they had a story to tell when they returned home. My dad was in charge and must have been a little concerned by the whole scene with all the lights, sirens, and trucks. Heck, I don't know. I was just a kid. Those were the days!

The Boys' Brigade is a Christian organization similar to the Boy Scouts. My dad ran one of the largest clubs in the country. He recruited and surrounded himself with men who cared about helping boys become good men—God's men. I would sometimes find it hard to fall asleep the night before Brigades while anticipating another exciting adventure.

We played sports together. Football, various forms of baseball, basketball, street hockey, steal the bacon, and whatever else we could dream up. We went exploring and camping at some pretty amazing places like Painted Canyon where we learned to enjoy and respect the outdoors. We set up camp, hiked, sat around the fire and of course goofed off in our tents at night. The flashlights were probably not always used as intended.

Back at the base, otherwise referred to by the adults as the church Fellowship Hall, we would have our weekly gatherings. These included pledging allegiance to the American and Christian flags, testings in our workbooks, indoor games, and various projects. As a brigade, we built a large fort structure out of popsicle sticks. It took us months so it's no wonder why our chests puffed when it was time for the big unveiling as parents and supportive congregants came to admire the edifice.

Competition, creativity, achievement, and encouragement were central to our core activities. We participated in team as well as individual contests. Tug-a-war was always one of my favorites. Everyone seemed to excel at something. We were discovering much about life, the world, and ourselves. A sense of belonging and achievement was experienced by all. It was the boy-man place to be.

Learning how to offer a firm hand shake while making good eye contact was encouraged, displayed, and practiced. Adding achievement patches to our well-pressed uniforms added validation for all our efforts. Saying "yes sir" and "no ma'am", learning how to use our Bibles, and cleaning up after our gatherings was all part of the culture.

Perhaps the most sustaining memories are from those who became your friends. Though each one of us came from unique homes and situations, at Brigade, we belonged. We were a team, a unit. We were a significant part of something important. I cherish these reflections more and more as I ponder the impact and influence this club had on so many young souls.

My dad, James William Piper, Sr., is the hero of this story. With four kids and a wife, a full-time job, and attending night school, he voluntarily built a program for boys. He built it like one who had a hundred hours a week to spare.

He and my beautiful mom (all my boyhood friends would tell me how beautiful she was) married young. Really young. Ten days after they married, dad headed off to the Navy's boot-camp while mom stayed with my dad's parents in Michigan.

Like many in those days, they started with love. Love was all they had in their bank account. They started with nothing but love and commitment toward one another. It was enough. It was plenty. My folks are the kind of people who create something out of nothing. As my long-time friend, Steve Dovey says, "Your folks are good people". They are. Plain and simple. They give. That's all they know. Together, they make good things and they make things good.

God made mankind, male and female. Mankind is not what it can be or what it was intended to be without both men and women. Do I really have to say this? Men can do a lot of things women can do and women can do a lot of things men can do yet God made us just different enough that we cannot live or thrive without each other. God knows what He is doing.

The Boys' Brigade taught me how to be a boy and as a result, it taught me what makes women different from me and what makes them special. Not less. Not more. It taught me admiration and respect. If I am an honorable man, I owe much of it to Mom, Dad, and the Boys' Brigade. For where I fail, I have little excuse. Hopefully, I will keep getting better.

While it seems that some in our world are making things more complicated, I am encouraged and confident God will continue to raise up people like Mom and Dad who will bring us back to the basics. For those who stray or feel like the world needs to be deconstructed, salt-of-the-earth kind of people will be in the kitchen baking apple pies and the aroma will draw folks back home.

Life Lesson: Some think to have convictions is to be divisive. If we were to adopt this kind of thinking, we must conclude that God is divisive. Instead, we must be people who seek, worship, and share the truth. If we do this with love in our hearts, we will learn from one another without betraying the truth.

There is plenty of evidence in this world to draw from to form our convictions. And there are subjects where there is room to grow and room to learn together. Yet, the truth is narrow. That's the very nature of truth. All sensible people desire truth because what does error provide?

In some cultures, people love their neighbors.
In other cultures, they eat them.

—Ravi Zacharias

> "Now the goal of our instruction is love from a pure heart, a good conscience, and a sincere faith."
>
> —1 Timothy 1:5, HCSB

From My Parents' Faith
to My Own

My parents modeled a life that made it difficult to deny the presence of God in our home. When compared to some of the homes of my teenage friends, *there was no denying the difference and this is no small part of how kids develop convictions* even if they are not readily realized.

There are no perfect guarantees but well-informed convictions align us with the nature of God. When we are aligned with God, we are showered with blessings. One of the blessings is courage. I see a significant relationship between courage and conviction. Though courage is revealed in the moment, it is simply the manifestation of deeply held convictions developed over the course of time.

Convictions are tested every day to varying degrees. Those that run deep and tempered will not buckle under pressure. They will reveal the moral authority and courage to overcome external pressures and influences. Developing your convictions will save your life and perhaps the lives of those you love and lead. It's never too late.

THE GIFT OF CONVICTION

Life experiences compound. As I explained in the previous chapters, adding to the influence of my parents, some of the values I have embraced were planted in my boyhood heart through my church and the Boys Brigade. If you do not have similar experiences, there is no need to feel short-changed.

While I am appreciative and blessed for such an upbringing, I still had to go through the process of filtering the faith of my parents into my own. As a very rational thinker, I questioned many tenets of the Christian faith from time-to-time during my younger years. I didn't just question some, I tested many of them and suffered the consequences. However, God's discipline is redemptive in nature. Even in His correcting, He gives life.

God's laws are built into the fabric of creation. You cannot escape them. They are not merely religious, they are reality. I wish I could tell you a wonderful story of complete and consistent devotion to God but that would be a worthless exercise. I am a logical person yet equally passionate. So, if I were to fake my story, you would know. They would have no life. I also cannot tell you a story of decades lost in darkness.

Perhaps my story is similar to yours. From my teen years through perhaps my mid-twenties, I was working hard to create a God of my own purposes. I wanted Him to be my genie, not my Lord. Even so, day-by-day, season-by-season, He brought me back into alignment. A delightful place to be for sure.

My rational side was never able to understand how anyone in their right mind could deny the existence of God. During the university years, Darwinism was thrown hard and fast in my face. The deductions made from his research and evolutionary theory—natural selection, seemed more like a leading question than an honest search for truth. My understanding of the disciplines of science includes a foundation of humility and curiosity. Once it begins making deductions without honest verification, it joins all other religions. It might as well be categorized as another religion.

Those who defend Darwin himself also claim Darwinsim has colored far outside the lines of the man himself. Nevertheless, once a person subscribes to a godless universe, power becomes the only rational end. Indeed, it will be survival of the fittest with no regard for right and wrong. There would be no right or wrong other than the spoils go to the victor! And in my estimation, that worldview has no regard for how one survives but simply survival itself becomes the moral high ground. From this worldview, anything that accomplishes survival is rational. Anything goes.

This brings me back to Christ. I cannot produce Jesus in the flesh. He is not staying in my guest room. I cannot say that I saw His resurrected body. I can't say we enjoyed lunch together this afternoon. I can't say any of those things or anything close. As a result, I have sometimes struggled to believe He was listening to my prayers. When I said jump, He did not jump.

I'm confident He remembers some of my adolescent prayers demanding He send an angel to visit me as a good faith gesture to win my affection and loyalty. Funny how we treat God as if He were shaking in His boots afraid that we won't believe in Him if He doesn't do what we want. Or as if He were an insecure teenager, needing the approval of others.

Yet, as a student of the Bible, it was extremely difficult, no, nearly impossible for me to walk away from the testimonies, history, prophecy, preservation, and validation of our copies, and the absolute wisdom and power that radiates off the pages of this book. The Bible says, God has placed eternity in the hearts of men. I take this to mean that we know there is more. We can't explain it but we just know it. This book also tells me that the heavens declare the glory of God. Now that's a no-brainer. The stars make my eyes well up. The ocean's roar is a constant reminder. The love for my family. The need to belong. The need for purpose. I could go on.

What evidence have I provided to support my convictions? I'm not sure that's my goal here. There were times in my life where I did not abandon my belief in God but I did doubt His level of involvement in our lives here on planet earth. To be more exact, I doubted His concern for my concerns. So, what did I do? I left my own counsel and sought the wisdom and experience of those who have gone before me. I read books with depth and authors of intellect far beyond my own. I studied. I put in the work. I sought after the truth. Over time, something amazing happened.

I stepped off God's throne.

I stepped off the throne. The one that said I was the boss. I was the center of the universe. Heck, I didn't even choose to be born. Who the heck am I? That's when I saw God on His throne. The next thing I learned and have been preaching ever since and will say again:

God is big enough to be small enough to care about you.

Life Lesson: Whether your childhood experiences have shaped you in one way or another, there is nothing that stops you from firmly establishing convictions of your own. I hope like me, you got a great headstart but if not, appreciate what you can and take heart, there is good in front of you. Pursue it with everything you have.

Love the Lord your God with all your heart, and with all your soul, and with all your mind, and with all your strength.

—Jesus of Nazareth

"

"Pain insists upon being attended to.
God whispers to us in our pleasures,
speaks in our consciences,
but shouts in our pains. It is his
megaphone to rouse a deaf world."

—C. S. Lewis

"

Pain Is a Teacher

I've had some really good teachers in my life. My parents, Coach Randy Rebold, Coach John Beresford, Dr. Mark Strauss, Dr. Lieth Anderson, and many others. Yet without a doubt, my most effective teacher has been Dr. Pain. I'm not referring to a person, I'm referring to pain itself. Not all of my lessons have come from pain but many have.

Pain is a symptom. Pain is a teacher. Pain is an amplifier blaring out a distracting noise. It screams, "Something is wrong!" Something is out of alignment. It is a protest, a proclamation, a confession, an SOS. Pain has a way of stopping your world, putting everything on hold. And it comes in many different forms or categories: physical, emotional, spiritual, relational, financial. If you have experienced significant physical pain, it illustrates to some degree what pain in any category can do.

THE GAME AND THE GAME OF LIFE

It was a shock. Perhaps the most physical pain I had ever experienced. I was a young man. Today, I would call myself a kid. Legally, I was a grown man, a husband and a father, and at the peak of my physical strength, speed, and confidence. As competitive as ever. I took it all for granted. I had left years of athletic training behind me and walked into the trap of becoming a weekend warrior. A person who traded their daily training and regular competition for a desk job and then weekend recreational competition.

It was a beautiful Sunday afternoon at the park, just around the corner from my home in Chino, California. A great day for basketball. Bill Durbin was bringing the ball down the court. A large man by most standards. The strength of his game was inside the paint, not the open court. Speed and quickness was my game. He was out in the open and I saw that as an opportunity to steal the ball and take it to the other end for an easy layup. The vision was clear but the results were much different.

In an awkward and freak collison, I experienced a jarring impact to my right shoulder. I fell to the ground, flat on my back. My arm lay next to me, useless. It was knocked clean out of place, out of alignment. My humerus bone, the rounded part at the top, was sitting completely outside the shoulder socket. I lay in agony. The pain would come and go as my muscles spasmed. I was feeling cold and my body went into shock.

The guys placed a blanket over me and dialed 9-1-1 because no one knew what to do. My son, about three or four years old at the time, saw all of this happening and began to gather twigs. Thinking his behavior was odd, one of our friends asked him what he was doing. His determined response: "Going to make my dad a fire. He is cold." That was the scene while we awaited the arrival of paramedics.

THE OTHER KIND OF PAIN

As wonderful as life can be, you experience moments and seasons when it's not. Those are the times when pain pleads for relief. It's when your relationship, your team, your world is out of alignment. You feel and see the reality of what is broken and you long for healing as fast as possible.

It feels like God is far away and indifferent. It's when your nightmare has come true. It's when your loved one cannot be reached. It's when you have been betrayed or when you have realized, you are the Judas. It's when your behaviors do not align with your intentions. It's when your relationships drain you instead of fill you. It's when you're sick and long for health. It's when your team members are combative. It's when you've lost a sense of purpose. It's when you fail.

THE ANTIDOTE TO PAIN

Alignment is more than the relief of pain. It is the ultimate place of peace, power, and speed. Peace is freedom from disturbance and the absence of war. Power is the ability to produce an effect. It's the sovereignty of purpose and productivity. Speed is the rate or measurement of how quickly something is accomplished.

JUST LIKE MY MUSTANG

The first car I bought with my own money was a 1964½ Ford Mustang. I was only eighteen. I paid $400 for the mess. Before I began restoring it, I learned that it was severely out of alignment. The effects of a car out of alignment are the exact opposite of peace. The car is at war within itself and its environment, it is unable to achieve desired speeds, and as a result, becomes less powerful and productive.

At certain speeds, the car would vibrate violently to the point where I would almost lose control until I took my foot off the accelerator and reduced speed. As soon as it hit about fifty miles per hour, the car felt like it was falling apart. It was difficult to steer. It seemed to fight me wanting to veer left. I would have to pull the steering wheel to the right just to keep it in the middle of my lane. Steering was especially difficult around corners and when braking. I also noticed extremely poor gas mileage and lots of exaggerated wear and tear on the tires, brakes, and other parts of the car. In that condition, the car was not fun to own or drive. So, I paid to have it aligned.

Everything changed once the car was aligned. It was a completely different experience. I was able to drive at high speeds, take corners without concern, and brake without veering in one direction or another. The alignment changed my frustrated state and motivated me to continue the restoration process. Eventually, she would receive a new exhaust system, paint job, tires and wheels, and a completely new interior. Alignment released more energy and faith to finish the work resulting in admiration from many car enthusiasts.

Alignment is like a barbershop quartet. Each vocalist has his part yet the whole produces a pleasant and balanced experience. Harmony. It doesn't happen without learning. It doesn't happen without cooperation. It doesn't happen without practice. It doesn't happen without appreciating differences. It doesn't happen without pain. It starts by recognizing you are not the center of the universe but you are an important part of something very special.

Life Lesson: Pain teaches us the priority of aligning our lives to what is right. The two broad categories of pain are: unnecessary and necessary. When we experience unnecessary pain, it is because of our own neglect or it is a result of living in a broken world. When we experience necessary pain, we are choosing acts of discipline and integrity that greatly reduce our exposure to unnecessary pain.

I ask myself these questions: Am I aligning my life to God's design? Am I aligning my body for its purposes? Am I working to align my relationships, behaviors, and work to the highest good? Am I aligning myself with the team?

PART II

THE PEOPLE THAT SHAPE US

"

"Think more about the person you
are and want to be
rather than what you want
to do or achieve."

—Jim Piper, Jr.

"

"
"But man's sin disordered all
relationships. Man was disordered
within his person, among his
persons, and in his relationship
with all of creation, because he
disordered his relationship
with God, upon which all other
relationships depend."

—P. A. Rizer

"

Well, That's That

I was eleven, the eldest of four. Our family drove from California to Tennessee to visit relatives. Dad, Mom, and us four kids: Jim, John, Robin, and Joe. During that stay, we went on a day trip and it became one of the oddest memories of my life.

We drove up to a homestead with two white structures—a detached garage and a small residence. It was the home of Grandpa Jimmy. Up to that day, I didn't know I had a grandpa named Jimmy. My memories of this event are more like a slideshow than a movie roll. I remember skinned rabbits hanging from the garage rafters, a quiet and awkward gathering in the living room, and the drive back.

Most significant is what I heard and felt as we pulled away from the awkward visit. Over the rumble of road noise, I heard my mom say to Dad, "Well, that's that." Her tone was simmering in sadness and unanswered questions seasoned with a pinch of acceptance and closure. Afterwards, the mood and spirit in the car was different. Much different. Instead of unceasing conversations along with four kids competing for space, it was quiet. When Mom was sad, the family mourned.

Decades earlier, Grandpa Jimmy left his wife and four daughters. The youngest, my mom, was a newborn still at the hospital. Grandma pulled herself up by her bootstraps and raised the four girls on her own. Mom told me she had an encounter or two with her father as she was growing up. One of those was when he was drunk and was trying to chase her out from under a bed with a broom. You get the picture. My mom grew up in a broken home. That's a problem.

Our story is not unusual. And that's the bigger problem. I call it our story because you cannot contain a person's sin within one house or one generation. We truly live in a broken world. I'm sure Grandpa Jimmy has a story of his own to tell. We all do but it doesn't take us off the hook. We are responsible for our decisions and actions.

NOW WHAT?

Why did Mom feel a need to face him after all those years? What did she imagine would come of it? She brought her family with her. Perhaps it would stir up something magical. Maybe he would come to his senses, ask forgiveness the best he knew how. God knows my mom would have responded with at least a measure of mercy. I don't know.

Sons and daughters, no matter how old they are, seek out estranged parents every day. It's in the blood. It's spiritual. It's the DNA, the family tree, the tribe. When it's violated, it's like planets colliding. We know it's not supposed to be this way. No matter how much psychologists want to help us make sense out of things, work through things, grasp realities and new possibilities, we just cannot escape the nightmare.

I grew up a little that day. I saw things. I felt things. I understood things. Things I did not realize until then. I knew Mom too well to see her as a victim yet my inner person shifted and my physical muscles flexed. I remember repeating those words in my head. Those exact words many times thereafter. Perhaps that's why I remember them to this day.

"Well, that's that." I was too young to realize that forgiveness was needed. Not because Grandpa Jimmy deserved it but because he didn't. He needed forgiveness because we all need it. I need it. Instead, my mind was on Mom. I didn't know how but I desperately wanted to remove her pain. I wanted to protect her like never before. If anyone raised their voice toward her, I was ready. I was on guard.

Even as a boy, I wanted to make things right for Mom. For all of us. I was void of this power but the desire was there. Once you realize you are not enough, that's when God's grace is realized in the strangest of ways.

We were already mourning and that is what we were supposed to do. Mourning is at the front end of the redemptive process. Being sad is an important emotion in the process of getting better. Being sad is not bad. We won't stay in that place forever but knowing it, feeling it, and coming back to it from time to time is more good than bad.

Unfortunately, some view sadness like sobriety in a culture that would rather be drunk or at least buzzed. You've heard the cliché, "Eat, drink, and be merry for tomorrow you die." The phrase has a ring of sadness to it but chooses not to think about it by indulging in gluttony. Anything to alter sadness. That's not the answer.

Sometimes it is unhealthy to forget. For example, our American culture struggles with the deeper meanings of holiday weekends meant to honor and remember the sacrifices made by others for our current benefit. We rush to them not so much to remember but to play. We just don't like to remember. We want to move on and get on with our lives.

The Jewish Passover meal is a great example of healthy remembering. Included in the meal, is a sampling of bitter herbs that serve to remind the Hebrew people of the suffering endured while enslaved by the Egyptians. And whether recognized or not, they remind us of the ministry of Jesus Christ. That's what Christian communion is all about. Remembering.

When you mourn the condition of humanity—now and all who have gone before us—you awaken the desire for change. King Solomon, considered one of the wisest who ever lived, wrote:

"Better to go to the house of mourning than to go to the house of feasting. For that is the end of all men; and the living will take it to heart."
Ecclesiastes 7:2, NKJV

When someone near us dies, our world stops. We ponder deep things. What happens when we die? What is the purpose of life? What matters most? Am I making the most of this life? Who do I want to be and what do I want to do?

BLESSINGS COME WITH MOURNING

Mourning is not static. It's not a psychological malfunction. It does not destroy like stepping into a pool of quicksand. Instead, it is cleansing and dynamic. When we mourn our condition and that of all mankind, we begin our redemptive journey and we are blessed in several transforming ways:

- *We are protected from stagnation caused by denial*

Mourning protects us from staying stuck. From remaining in a state of denial that all will go on as it has. We are protected from lying to ourselves. Small problems turn into big problems when we deny they exist. Small errors in thinking grow larger and have the power to destroy us when they are not examined, recanted, and corrected.

- *We are in a place where God can reach us*

Scripture teaches us that God lifts up the humble yet He resists the proud. Simply put, some people refuse to see their need for help. They choose to take on life alone. They are self-reliant. Those who see their brokenness desire restoration. Those are the kind of people God can help.

- *We will be comforted*

In Jesus' famous sermon found in the fifth chapter of Matthew, He begins with these words: "Blessed are the poor in spirit (when someone realizes they need God), For theirs is the kingdom of heaven. Blessed are those who mourn, For they will be comforted."

There is a supernatural awakening and strengthening for those who move from being man-centered to God-centered. Our redemption begins by recognizing that we can do nothing apart from God.

Life Lesson: The bad things in our lives do not have the power to ruin us unless we let them. In fact, they can be woven together within our life's story transforming us into better humans. Let's be stubborn toward the good even when the good does not always feel like it should.

"My grandfather was
a wonderful role model.
Through him I got to know
the gentle side of men."

—Sarah Long

Grandpa Piper

I once heard a teacher describe God in complementary terms: mother heart and father heart. At first, I was bothered because I had never thought of God in feminine terms. Afterall, the Christian faith uses the masculine pronoun when referring to God. Jesus taught us to pray, "Our Father who art in Heaven". And of course, Jesus was male. However, the more I thought about the masculine and feminine concepts for God's nature, the more it made sense.

As we recall, humankind was made in the image of God, male and female. The implication is clear. Humanity necessarily animates the image of God through both sexes. The prophet Isaiah compares God's affection for his people like a mother's love.[1] The Apostle Paul describes his ministry to the church in Thessalonica like a mother caring for her children.[2]

Men and women, together, add tremendous value to our families, houses of worship, ministry, business, and society as a whole. Each adds unique value to the development of children, especially when we work to partner both innate and nurtured strengths. One sex is obviously no less valuable than the other. Mature

---

[1] Isaiah 49:15-16
[2] I Thessalonians 2:7-8

masculinity and femininity promote the image of our creator.

CROOKED NAILS

Some people have a long impact on your life even if their actual time with you was short. That was the case with my grandpa. Born in Cornwall, England, he left as a young man to experience employment stints in Brazil and South Dakota working in the mines. He eventually made his way into marriage and fatherhood while landing in the suburbs of Detroit. He served in the U.S. Army during WWI, lived through the Depression, and retired from Burroughs, the adding machine company. After retiring, he, Grandma, and Aunt Jean moved to be near us in southern California. The year was 1967.

Grandpa's dominating talent was making the organ come alive. If a church organ sound popped into your head just now, that's not what I am trying to describe. Oh yes, he could do the church organ thing with the best of them. What he could also do was leave you speechless. He did things on those keys you've never heard before. Trust me. I think the organ itself was shocked with what it could do at the hands of a master. If you could hum a few notes, he'd take it from there while you watched and listened with your mouth wide open in both amazement and delight.

You could not resist the man. Not like a clown or flamboyant persona but like a magnet. He was a magnet. There was a gentle way about him that pulled you into his orbit. Often, he would invite me to squeeze up next to him in his chair. Then he would seize the moment by reaching under his chair and pull out his lapdesk. As he lifted the lid, he would sneak out two pieces of his secret stash. Peanut brittle. One for him; one for me. We would quietly savor the morsels like two criminals hiding in the shadows. We were trying to avoid the mini-lecture from Grandma about spoiling our supper.

On that lapdesk, he would make the world come alive with just a pencil and piece of paper. I was constantly amazed as I watched him transform a blank canvas into a scenic view of mountains, trees, and streams. Sketching portrait-like images of various species of birds seemed to be his favorite. Our family tells stories of the days in Michigan when a bird would fly back every spring to sit near Grandpa as if to have an annual reunion with a dear friend.

In his workshed, he would teach. He taught me how to measure and cut. He demonstrated how to pull nails out of hardwoods using a variety of angles and leverage points. He would show me how to straighten out an old bent nail so it could be useful again. We would toss those straightened nails into the repurposed coffee can, designated for nails only.

Grandpa died in 1973 when I was thirteen. They said it was cancer, but we all knew it was from a broken heart. Grandma had passed earlier due to injuries she sustained in an automobile accident. They were rear ended by a truck while sitting in their car at a traffic light. After Grandma was gone, he just wasn't the same. There is an invisible power we gain and lose through certain relationships.

I didn't connect the dots at the time. I was too young. But the times we spent in his workshed were history lessons of his years as a carpenter working with timber in the mines. It was a reminder of the Depression when it was not a waste of time to pull nails, straighten them, and reuse them another day.

What Grandpa may not have known, is that he didn't waste his time by investing in me. He saw me and I saw him. Since those days, I've struggled to throw nails away. Everytime I see a nail, especially an old crooked one, I have an urge to tap it back into shape and set it aside for another day. Everytime I see an organ, a piece of peanut brittle, or a crooked nail, I think of Grandpa.

We should draw closer to those from generations past. While the younger generation feels, sees, and experiences the present and maybe some of the future, it is short on context. Yesteryear is the foundation for today.

I might not be able to play the organ like Grandpa but a little smirk appears in my heart when I witness a rare musician adding a unique lick to those keys. She doesn't know it but her keyboard connects me to memories of Grandpa.

I shouldn't eat too much peanut brittle. It's tough on the teeth and has a lot of sugar. Today, there are varieties of peanut brittle. It's no longer controlled by the peanut. Other nuts have been invited to the party: cashews, pecans, and almonds. That's just a short list. I find it difficult to walk out of a shop without savoring a piece or purchasing a small package for later. When I do, it propels me back on that chair, sneaking a piece before Grandma catches us!

I may never hammer one of those restored nails. I just don't work with my hands that much. However, I have caught myself on more than one occasion teaching my son or one of my grandkids how to straighten a nail. When I do, I'm sure to tell them about Grandpa.

Never once have any of them showed a disinterest in their heritage. When they see their connection to the past, they see greater meaning for their present and their future. Grandpa's life mattered, and so does theirs.

Life Lesson: Surround your kids with elders who will love them. Surround yourself with mentors. Let these souls provide the gifts of belonging, calm, and wisdom. Maybe it's a grandfather or maybe a grandmother. Maybe it's the patriarch or matriarch of your church or community. It's difficult to center yourself without the help of those who have grown wise and loving.

"

"Life gives you no guarantees.
But I know one thing: if you sell out
and lose, it will mean more to you
than if you go through the motions
and win. It's not about what you
get at the end. It's about how
you choose to live the pursuit."

—Sherri Coale

"

Side by Side

PING PONG

It's late on a summer evening and the single- car garage door is open providing some much needed relief from the heat. The competition is fierce. The space is tight. It's mano a mano as in hand-to-hand combat or one-on-one. The more experienced and wise father VS the enthusiastic, never-tiring, mistakes galore yours truly. The game: ping pong, otherwise known by the olympic committee as table tennis.

Back and forth we would go late into the night even though Dad's work started at 8 AM sharp. Having the obvious advantage, Dad chuckles when his son returns his tricky serves or makes the unexpectant power shot right down the line while barely able to see over the table. In the early years, I never expected to win, but I did set internal goals about how many points I would score. Once that goal was achieved, I'd set another goal and then another. Add a few years, and there was a serious game going. They were nail biters. So entertaining, we would sometimes draw a small crowd of onlookers from the neighborhood.

There was laughter, challenges, arguments. Witnesses would sometimes have to referee. This was serious stuff. Who was king of the table? Fortunately, the game had its built-in commercial breaks when we struggled to find that wayward ball. It would bounce into toolboxes, under chairs, on top of the highest shelving, and eventually, sooner or later, find its demise.

Sometimes it would be accidentally stepped on or cracked by a powerful overhead slam thus becoming useless. There was a short life expectancy for each of these balls but sometimes they just died of natural causes. The ping pong ball was a precious commodity indeed. There was an extra measure of reverence and honor for the last survivor whenever we realized there were no more backups. As fate would have it, some nights would come to a sad, sudden, and dramatic ending.

It wasn't just ping pong. It was me standing at the plate while Dad threw one pitch after another. He would throw overhand and sidearm. He would throw fast balls, change ups, sucker pitches, and whatever else he had up his sleeve. As my siblings grew, they would join in the games. When we played football, Dad would be the quarterback for both teams. We would also play cowboys and indians. Whatever the game or make-believe activities, if Dad was home, you'd find him in the midst.

Many families have holiday traditions, ours is no exception. We play football. When it was the original four and much younger, tackle football was the game. Today, it's flag. Sometimes at Thanksgiving; other times, Christmas. Whoever is present for the gathering plays. If you can walk, you're in. If you can't walk very well any more, you're in. Someone gets hurt almost every year. If the injury is not physical, it's emotional. I'm pretty sure winning is a core value for this tribe.

When someone gets hurt emotionally, there is a delay but they usually duct tape themselves together and get on with it. When the injury is physical, the game comes to a screeching halt. We rush in gathering around to make sure he or she will survive. If it appears they won't die, we pick them up and set them on the sidelines. Sixty seconds later, the game resumes. These holiday football games have been played in multiple cities in California, Oregon, Washington, Colorado, and Texas.

For me, the ideas and gifts of athletics, competition, self-improvement, leadership, teamwork, encouragement, camaraderie, family, and friends, all started in that single-car garage arena. It started with a father who was all in. It started with the simple things. A table, two paddles, and a ping pong ball. But there's even a bigger lesson here.

Over my lifetime, I've noticed side-by-side conversations are much more powerful than the formal face-to-face. Most of what I have learned from my father came while we were living life doing whatever we were doing. Working, playing, running errands, solving practical problems, dealing with neighbors, dealing with loss. These are the places and events one does not soon forget. Lectures and formal conversations are less effective. They come from the top-down manager mindset. It's the old-school style and it's not effective.

Side-by-side is what my folks did so well. It's how I captured a strong work ethic. Heck, all of my siblings work their tails off. I've never needed anyone to remind me I should be working. I love to work. It's almost as fun as ping pong. It's all in or not in. This all-in ethic comes from my parents. If you want to see a clean and organized home, find my mom and you will experience it. If you are looking for a woman of impeccable character, find my mom.

My room was clean. Always clean and organized. Most of the years I shared it with both brothers. I do not remember lectures. I remember culture. She set the bar, we watched, and we followed.

Today I advise leaders to practice side-by-side leadership with less formality and certainly less power moves. I encourage them to see their team members more often. To be physically present and to move. Literally, move. Take a walk, paint a fence, and play pickleball. I don't care what it is, move. Life and leadership is about movement. Try it.

If you model office leadership behind your desk, that's the culture you will create. Bosses sit behind desks. Bosses call you into their office. It's stagnant and formal. It's not really human if you think about it. I have a desk to write on, maybe read on, and maybe for planning purposes. My desk does not create authentic communication. It creates distance.

Life & Leadership Lesson: If I have learned anything about leading others over my lifetime, I've noticed that when leaders are engaged with their teams, the team is energized. However, if the leader backs off a little, the team tends to back off a lot. Leadership works better when it is up close and personal.

"The influence of one good human being is immeasurable."

—John Quincy Adams

From Leper to Leader

I was awakened out of a trance-like state by a standing ovation. I was just a kid. At the moment, I was out-of-touch with my current physical surroundings because I was busy imagining being a leper who needed healing. I was performing a re-enactment of a biblical story in front of a building filled with parents, teachers, and faculty at some sort of regional competition. As I ended, I was literally startled by the response of the crowd, I didn't even remember walking out on stage.

Weeks before, I'm reading the story off two double-sided sheets of notebook paper. The narrative was someone's re-creation of a New Testament story when Jesus heals a leper. I read the story over and over again. Worn out from the folding and unfolding, day after day, tears replaced creases. After weeks of abuse, the notes looked more like pieces of large confetti than lined notebook paper.

Next came time to recite the story without the aid of notes. Again and again. Again. It is not enough to robotically regurgitate the written words. It must become grafted into the brain so that each word can be transformed into something more. Mom had me recite the story over and over until she was convinced it was memorized, unable to escape my mind.

Every word and punctuation mark was now under the microscope. Exegeting meaning and emotion from every phrase. Voice fluctuations, pauses, silence, facial expressions, body language, and eye movements are now added to the recitals.

Adjustments and repairs in front of a mirror became part of the preparation. Getting it exact was not good enough. It had to be human, grimy, smelly, even painful. It had to be better than believable, it must transport all who watch and listen to the early years of first-century Jerusalem. Small imperfections were purposefully placed to accomplish the integrity of the moment. A stutter carefully positioned would draw in the listener.

THE LEPER

I had to become the leper. I was the leper.

Secretly, all this work to become the incarnated leper of this story resonated with me. Even as a little boy, I sometimes felt like a leper. I was small. Most of my friends were a head taller than me. Though I was years away from adolescence, my insecurities were beginning to take root.

Things just got worse as I approached those roller coaster teens. I definitely started noticing girls. I was picky, even if most of the relationships were a figment of my imagination. My hair was troublesome. I still have those pesky cowlicks though not near as honorary as they once were. A thinning crop up top and a pair of deepening cul-de-sacs help solve most of that problem.

Probably most troubling was my love and inborn skill to compete at sports while largely being ignored by those in the world of organized athletics. Though I was a well-known commodity in the neighborhood, I was literally overlooked by the school or club teams or at least until they dragged an injured player off the field. All of this changed when one teacher/coach noticed me.

COACH RANDY REBOLD

Coach Randy Rebold never asked permission, he just did it. He affectionately nicknamed me Pipe. I was shocked when he put me in the starting lineup of the basketball team. I was shocked when he started me as middle linebacker and kick-off return man on the flag football team. To top it all off, he put me as the starting second baseman in front of the more popular one, my beloved cousin. What in the world was happening?

All the while enjoying the fame of being an eighth grade all-star athlete at school, I was informed by my buddies that a beautiful girl was taking notice of me. Peggy had long, very long, straight, jet black hair. As the romance developed from afar, we found ourselves sitting together at the lunch table. And then it happened.

She leaned over and gave me a slow and mean- ingful kiss on the cheek in front of the whole table. As

I tried to take it in stride, my blushing face gave me away. I knew this could be grounds for detention or suspension or something sinister like that. Kissing at a Christian school was a serious offense.

But not this day. Right on time, witnessing the evil act, Coach Randy walked by and gave me a wink. And so the dream year continued. I was having the time of my life. Intercepting passes, running kick-offs back for touchdowns, making shots on the court I never knew I could, and making a few plays out on the sandlot as a bonus. It was one of the best years of my young life. When spring was turning to summer and school was wrapping up for the year, it was time for the awards assembly.

Coach called me up to receive the best all-around-athlete-of-the-year award. It was the cherry on top of a memorable year. Everyone was so kind and happy for me. How did they know this was just what I needed? I needed to be seen.

One person can change the world for a kid. I don't know why Coach started calling me Pipe but it gave me a new identity. A fresh start. I became the little-big man on campus even if it was just for one year of a boy's life, it set the stage for what was yet to come.

I think a lot of us feel like a leper once in a while. I know I did. Maybe it was Jesus who sent Coach Rebold to heal my inner leprosy. Maybe my story is why I tend to root for the underdog. To see kids achieve and smile. To see people overcome. Maybe my experience is why I enjoy watching everyday people have their year. The year that changes the rest of their life.

Life & Leadership Lesson: Every person you come in contact with has a story and you have the ability to help shape it for good. So, be careful to notice people and take an interest in who they are. Maybe you will become Coach Randy Rebold to someone someday. And what could be better than that?

"

"Competitive Greatness is not
defined by victory nor denied by
defeat. It exists in the effort that
precedes those two "imposters" as
well as their accomplices: fame,
fortune, and power—measurements
of success I rejected long ago."

—Coach John Wooden

"

Making a Comeback

Maybe you are one of the few. You've never been in a ditch. You've never had to hustle to get your grades up. You've never been behind on your sales quota. You've never had to will yourself back to health. You've never had to fight to save your marriage. You've never had to work to get your house out of foreclosure. You've never had to start again. Well, if you're one of those, you can skip to the next chapter because this one is not for you!

ROD HENDRY

There was really only one way to wrestle Rod Hendry. You had to become tougher and more stubborn than you thought you could. You had to become a boulder of a man inside and out because that's what it was like going head-to-head with the guy. Stocky, hard, sweaty, persistent, and tough. Those words paint the picture of who he was on the mat.

Winter 1977, three young men accomplished their individual and collective wrestling goals by becoming conference champions. Those youngsters, yours truly, Rod Hendry, and Dan Grant became high school buddies that year as they trained together and traveled across southern California competing in dual meets, round robins, and open tournaments. We were busy sharpening our craft with one goal in mind, becoming champions.

While on the journey, we talked about wrestlers and wrestling. We talked about life and we talked about God. We became more than teammates, we became friends. And when we walked off the mat as champions that winter, we felt a great sense of accomplishment assuming more good times were just around the corner.

Then everything changed. Dan said he was not coming back to the team for his senior year. His decision was not popular and broke up the trio. Then came Guillain-Barre' Syndrome.

Rod was in the hospital, unconscious, and fighting for his life. It seemed to come out of nowhere. There was talk that he may not live and if he did, he would not walk or run and certainly never wrestle again. It seemed like it all happened in a day. While Dan was moving on to different things, Rod was hanging on by a thread, and I was lost.

Guillain-Barre' Syndrome essentially is when the body attacks itself and the nervous system. To put it in sloppy layman's terms, the body wages war against the wrong enemies and therefore throws itself into chaos. Like many conditions, viruses, or reactions to germs and infections, there are common and uncommon symptoms. They can range from mild episodes to death. In Rod's case, it was critical and wasn't looking good.

To me, Rod was a big man, inside and out. He was one of very few friends who was actually shorter than me yet his personality, character, and work ethic made him seem taller. He filled space but never in a boisterous or flashy kind of way. I think it had to do with his energy. His humor yet sincerity. His optimism yet his vulnerability. I guess that's why it was difficult to believe that he was in serious trouble.

We didn't have mobile phones in those days. We didn't have email. We didn't have social media. So, local communication was done word-of-mouth or by telephone. The kind of telephone plugged into the wall of your home or office. Staying up-to-date with Rod's condition was not easy. We did our best but mostly prayed and waited for news.

Rod and I lived in the mountain community of Crestline, California. There were a couple ways to get to my house off of the main drag. One of those routes took you past Rod's place. As I was making my way through the winding roads, I decided to make that hard and steep right hand turn that would take me by Rod's house on the way to mine. I just wanted to drive by. I had no practical reason, maybe just a bit of sadness and curiosity wooed me in that direction.

As I approached the Hendry's property up the road and to the right, Rod's little blue truck was parked in its typical spot but someone was standing in the bed of the truck. As I slowed down in curiosity to see who might be sweeping pine needles out of the bed, the person stood up straight and looked me in the eyes. It wasn't until then that I was able to identify the stranger.

It was Rod! I didn't recognize him because he was significantly heavier with a puffy face full of acne. He obviously recognized me right away, waving as I drove by. I stopped, put the jeep in reverse and got out. It was a delayed reaction on my part that created a bit of awkwardness. I was caught off guard and didn't know what to say. We spoke for a brief moment but I don't remember what was said. It was different. I don't know how else to describe it.

I couldn't wait to tell my folks. I was happy, shocked, and concerned. As emotion settled into thought, I wasn't sure the guy I had just talked to was the Rod I knew. Or was he?

School was already in session for me. Rim of the World High School was year round at the time. Students were assigned tracks when they would be in school and on break. No one went the traditional nine months in school and then out for summer. It was broken up into smaller chunks. As a result, the whole of the student body was never in school at the same time. This complicated communication and relationships even more.

Talk about Rod at school was like any community, some accurate and some dead wrong. Would he ever come back? Is he the same? How is he different? What should we say or do if he does come back? I didn't know what to think and I didn't know what to do. I waited.

Here's what happened. Step by step, day by day, Rod mounted a comeback. And what a comeback it was. As our class vice-president, honor student, athlete, wrestling champion, and friend, he was always inspiring. Now, he was more. His battle for normalcy was on full display. I believed he would overcome and get back to a normal and healthy life. I did not believe he would ever wrestle again. I was wrong.

When he walked back into the wrestling tunnel, I wondered why. I was endeared to him even more than before but I didn't know how to approach. It was still awkward. Looking back, I think it was a mixture of my lack of interpersonal skills and his seen and unseen encumbrances.

Slowly but surely the old Rod was making his move. Come to think of it, the new Rod was making his move. However, like in most sports, what you accomplished in the past has little to do with today. Rod struggled to stay on his feet. He was getting beat by lesser wrestlers but he just kept showing up. It had to be frustrating. His balance was off, his strength and speed were not what they were. His physical endurance was obviously missing. Those of us who knew him, loved him, were rooting for him.

Day by day, his weight began to move toward normal. His strength, balance, and endurance came rushing back. There was a new inner drive even greater than his past. One by one, his opponents fell. He was back on varsity and the war continued. Winning at that level was tough after what he had been through. Point by point, match by match, the comeback continued. Could he possibly qualify for the tournament?

He did. He won and then moved on to southern sections. He advanced. His comeback carried him deep into the championships much farther than he had ever done before. He did it. The old Rod was back and the newer version was better than the previous. After high school we would get together from time to time. Mostly centered around sports, we moved into adulthood as friends with a story dear to us both.

Today, Rod operates his own financial consulting business in one of the popular and affluent desert communities of southern California. We don't talk as much as we once did but he will always be my friend and I will always be proud of what he did. He did not settle, he rose up and made a comeback. His story has served as a shaping tool in my life. For little did I know how much this experience would prepare me for things to come.

Life & Leadership Lesson: You can't get through life without trouble. No one in their right mind wants it but when it comes, what turns it from bitter to sweet is when you rise up, look it in the eye, and then go at it. Like Joseph, Moses, and Peter, God will give you the strength to make a comeback if you so choose. Frankly, I'm not sure you can accomplish noble things without having some comeback stories along the way.

> "I always challenged our teams to play in such a way that people walking to their cars when the game was over would say to themselves, 'I want to be a better me' "

—Hall-of-Fame Coach Sherri Coale

I Want to Be a Better Me

Every once in a while you meet a soul who just seems to be better than the rest of us. Jim Ramos was one such person. The people in his life called him Dad, Jim, Jimmy, and Ramos. I met him the summer between my junior and senior year of high school. I was looking for a family that would take me in for my last year of high school.

My dad accepted a promotion that required us to relocate. After some private conversations, my folks unselfishly provided a couple of options. I could move with my family or I could stay and finish my last year at Rim of the World High School in Lake Arrowhead, California. If I chose to stay, we would need to agree on the specifics.

I was one of the captains of the wrestling team, had a good job, a partnership in a firewood business, and a few but significant friendships. We began to spread the word that I was an orphan of sorts and that's when we heard about a youth pastor at a local Calvary Chapel who might be interested in helping us.

One afternoon, both of our families met at Jim's house to discuss the arrangement. As I recall, that was about all it took and the deal was done. The next nine months or so ushered in an amazing season of new perspectives and relationships.

I became an addition to a family of four, Jim and his wife Joann, and their two young children, Lee and Malia. Jim and Joann knew their way around the kitchen. Jim was the Executive Chief at Calvary Chapel Conference Center and Bible College located in Twin Peaks, California. Their mountain cabin was walking distance from the conference center with its landscaped grounds, recreational facilities, camp-style rooms, dining hall, and meeting spaces. It was a mountain oasis.

As an addition to the Ramos family, I was received with open arms by conference center staff which seemed to operate much like a large family. In our crowded and busy world, kindness is a hard thing to miss. It oozed out of Jim as natural and soothing as a mountain spring. He knew everyone's name. He remembered their stories, their likes and dislikes. His face and energy came alive as soon as he saw you. His kindness filled the culture.

He was busy. Busy serving. Preparing meals, running errands, taking inventory, cleaning, teaching, and laughing. Always laughing. He was up early and when evening came, he served to the point of exhaustion. He had given his all. If there is a person easy to like and easy to love, his name is Jim Ramos.

When you join another family, you end up in the same river of activities and relationships. The Ramos family attended Calvary Chapel, Twin Peaks (Calvary, for short) which congregated inside the main hall of the conference center. They did church much differently than my family. Calvary's culture was a radical contrast from what I was used to. In my family's tradition, we dressed up, sang out of hymnals, followed an order of service, and listened to a preacher, followed by an altar call much like what you would expect at a Billy Graham crusade.

Calvary Chapel was different, much different. It was birthed during the Jesus Movement, what many would recall as the hippie days. The music was led by a guitarist sitting on a stool and the vibe was laid back, similar to a prayer or love song. Many in attendance were wearing shorts, T-shirts, and sandals. The preaching was not preaching. It was not a prepared sermon with three points and a call to action. It was a verse-by-verse commentary from the Bible. The pastor simply started from where he left off the previous week. I was curious, confused, and guarded all at the same time.

Midweek, the teenagers gathered in the Ramos home. One or two would bring guitars and they would lead the group in singing Christian songs, most of which I had never heard before. The room was packed and the singing was intense. There seemed to be a genuine faith and love expressed toward God and one another. Jim would teach from an open Bible and an open heart. We could feel it and he captured our attention. It wasn't his oratory skill, it was his common sense laced with love and sincerity.

I began inviting some of my wrestling friends to the youth gatherings. After the organized portion of the evening was over, we would move the furniture around for some tag team wrestling entertainment. I think we were just trying to show off in front of the girls. Somehow, we convinced Jim to be one of our volunteer participants. He would outwardly protest but in the end, he was right in the middle of the action. Sometimes the wrestling would spill outside into the snow, adding a new dimension to the sport. Fortunately, other than the rug burns and an occasional black eye, no one was seriously injured.

I wasn't a bad kid but I did not always make it easy on the Ramos family. I had racked up some sizable long distant phone bills with all the calls I made to my girlfriend. Rhonda lived down the mountain in San Bernardino. We had met at my previous church and we were becoming a thing. I was also without a car for a while. I blew up the engine because I failed to check the oil levels in spite of my dad's constant coaching. Jim allowed me to borrow his car from time-to-time to drive down the mountain. To make a long story short, that resulted in worn out tires due to my driving speeds around those winding mountain roads. And I can't leave out mentioning the fender bender.

I came walking up the drive one day and saw someone having what looked like a serious conversation with Jim and Joann. The three were standing by the parked cars when they heard my feet shuffle up the drive. When Jim saw it was me, he motioned toward me with one arm and said, "There he is, ask him for yourself." It was a social worker from Child Protective Services. The representative looked at me with a motherly smile that quickly transformed into an inquisitive and serious expression.

She asked me if I was being mistreated in any way by any person living in the home. She saw my puzzled look and added that she was responding to concerns from a neighbor about screaming and crying coming from the house on various evenings. The neighbor added another clue. The voices seemed older than a little child, thus their concern for me, a seventeen-year-old. Once I realized what was happening, I failed to grasp the seriousness of the situation and let out some laughter.

I explained to the official about the sounds. They were not coming from me, they were coming from Jim. I used him to practice all of my wrestling moves and sometimes my friends and I would tickle him or even give him a pink belly. Sound carries well in the mountains, that's for sure. I can see how easy it can be for innocent people to get in trouble.

Jim had a significant and positive influence on my life. I could not think of anyone I'd rather have to officiate my wedding to Rhonda just a few years later. He took us through some premarital education prior to the big day but I think most of it went over our heads.

We were young and determined to blaze our own trail no matter what.

Jim stepped into eternity not long ago while still serving at another Calvary in Hawaii. He came down with a sudden health event and left us before we could say goodbye, until next time. I miss him and his radiation of goodness.

Life & Leadership Lesson: Leadership starts with being the kind of person the world needs. Generous, kind, honest, and hard-working. Who can protest such qualities? This man taught me what comes first before anything else.

"He who finds a wife finds a good thing and receives favor from the Lord. "

—Proverbs 18:22

That Girl

To say we were just kids is an understatement. The first time I saw her, she was attending my high school youth group. She was sporting green corduroys with a hairbrush stuffed in her back pocket. She caught my eye, that's for sure. It was her looks and something else. It was her wavy dark hair, the sparkle in her eyes and her energy. But the grand prize winner was her laugh.

If you asked me what attributes I love most about my wife, I would have a long list. For now, I'll give you a short one: loyalty, discipline, diligence, faithfulness, truth-teller, hard worker, self-sacrificing, love for life, and her wounds.

It might sound strange for me to include her wounds in a list of coveted attributes. It shouldn't. Her wounds give her depth. And they are a holy ground kind of place where I have been allowed to enter. She is an overcomer and a winner for sure.

It doesn't matter where we are or what I am doing. If I hear her laugh, I stop. If I am not near her, I search for her to see what she is laughing about. She has a unique sense of humor and finds certain things really funny. She doesn't hold back. She lets it out. Her laugh amplifies joy and freedom. I cannot count how many times I have sat through a comedy consumed by her laughter. I have found it much more enjoyable than the movie or the performance itself. Her laugh is one of those gifts from God that just keeps on giving.

No doubt about it. Rhonda's laugh is my favorite thing. Well, maybe it's my second favorite thing. At the time I am writing this, we've been a married couple for nearly forty-four years. Maybe that's my favorite thing. She's truly my best friend.

OUR FIRST CHAPTER

It was a brand new one-bedroom apartment. We moved in with an ice chest to serve as our refrigerator, a bench press serving as a tv stand, a thirteen-inch television, a box spring and mattress set, and a variety of household items gifted at our wedding reception. We had a used but very clean Pontiac and a moped resting in the carport. We were playing house and we loved it.

We were both taking college classes and working. She worked at a diner and hardware store. I worked at the town's newspaper, *The Hemet News*. I was the circulation manager. In other words, a glorified paperboy. I hired paperboys, trained them, and dropped off stacks of papers for them to fold and deliver. There was more to the job but I found it pretty simple and it paid the bills.

Shortly after our marriage, opportunity came knocking. I had multiple job offers and was undecided. I was experiencing a little anxiety about making the wrong choice. Today, they call that FOMO, the Fear

Of Missing Out. The newspaper offered a substantial pay increase to stay, General Telephone offered incredible benefits but I would have to serve one year as a telephone operator before choosing one of their many career paths, and Bank of America offered me a management trainee position that entailed twelve months of training culminating into a bank officer position.

As much as we appreciated the offer from the newspaper's ownership, the Gill family, we quickly narrowed our decision between the bank and the telephone company. Here comes the embarrassing part. I lied to the phone company in order to keep both opportunities in play just in case I didn't like the bank after a month or so. Over the phone, I told the telephone company's hiring manager that I had broken my leg as a result of an auto accident and asked if I could start at a later date. She kindly informed me that I could still be an operator with a broken leg. I reacted with another lie. I told her one of my arms had also been broken during the crash. It's interesting how one lie can give birth to many more lies.

There was an awkward moment of silence. She knew I wasn't telling the truth and I felt like an idiot. I was an idiot. She kindly encouraged me to call when I was ready to go to work. I did call. Several weeks later, my conscience drove me to eat humble pie, confess, and apologize. She gave me the same advice my mom has always given. In the long run, telling the truth serves us better.

Through the years, I've done some not-so-smart things that have probably caused my wife to pause. I've also accomplished some things she doubted was possible. Through it all, she has been my ever-present partner.

As we learned how to live together and become one, not just two individuals dwelling in the same space, we started making decisions together. To do this well, we had to stop and observe one another. We had to learn how to listen because we began to realize there was much we didn't know about each other. That's the beauty of the journey. Even now after more than four decades of marriage, I still learn new things about my bride.

We started blocking time for marriage business. We discussed things important to us that the other probably didn't realize. We discussed how we would handle money. How we would decide what the next financial goal would be. How much we would save, give to the church, other ministries, and for friends and family in need.

We noticed how young couples were accumulating tons of debt buying nice things and stacking up unthinkable student loans. We opted out of that path. So, we decided that I would go to school and Rhonda's employment would be used in part to keep us out of debt. We don't view my degrees as mine. We earned them together; therefore, they are ours.

We talked about how we wanted to be treated in front of others. We noticed early on that sometimes we would unknowingly hurt the other's feelings in social settings. We realized we both had a measure of insecurity. We were sensitive and expected more from our spouse. So, we made rules and when we followed them, we were buddies.

We had to learn new ways of relating to our extended families. Every couple does. We had honest and difficult conversations about how to navigate the complicated and sometimes hurtful past, current day expectations, and when we felt over-looked. Looking back, we had a whole lot of physical energy but not-so-much maturity. We have grown together to be better participants in our collective family.

We were married young so we decided to wait five years before having children. Some might see this decision as playing God. I have mixed feelings about it today. If I have regrets, I wish we would have had more children. We have always enjoyed being parents and now that we are grandparents, the joy is almost unbearable.

Our first child was never born. He died in the womb. I remember every detail of those days. We knew something was wrong. The long hour-plus drive to the doctor. The drive back with no clear answers but bedrest orders. The long and quiet drive home, tucking her into bed. The drive back to the office.

As I began the descent into my office chair, my assistant answered an incoming call. It was one of those moments when everything goes into slow motion. As she turned toward me, the look on her face said it all. I left the bank office as fast as I came. The rest is too graphic and unnecessary to describe. It was a defining moment for us. It sunk in. Bad things, really bad things, happen to us all.

I still get choked up. Even now, emotions get the better of me. They race past my typing fingers falling heavy into my heart. It is difficult for me to relive those moments. They are a mixture of powerpoint slides and video reels playing in my head. It was more than physical for her. It was also emotional. Both wrapped up in pain, disbelief, and confusion.

In the moment, I did what I had to do. In between, I cried like a baby. I mostly hid my pain. I didn't know what to do. I had never experienced this before. I felt guilty and weak.

Look what my girl has gone through. This was my recurring thought. I felt tremendous loss and I felt powerless. It was thirty-nine years ago.

There is good in this story. It's difficult to explain but when a man and woman come together in sincere matrimony, they really do become one. We lost a child. She went through physical pain and loss only a mother can understand. That is her unique position as a woman—one who carries the image of God in her bosom. I went through a sense of failure and guilt. I did this to her. It might sound irrational to you but these were my feelings. I am a husband-father-protector who carries the image of God in my bosom. We lost a child. It's the WE that squeezes the good out of this story. We don't split apart, we come together more than ever.

Jim III was born in July of 1985 and Mandy Sue in May of 1988. Together with their spouses (whom we love dearly and consider our own), have blessed us with seven grandchildren. If you're a parent, you understand how difficult it is to describe this kind of love. It's joy-filled, sorrowful, tender, tough, devastating, worry-filled. Let's face it. Love is painful. I cannot fully describe the love I have for my family but it sure helps me believe and embrace the love God must have for each of us.

As much as we love and enjoy our entire family, we have nurtured our marriage above all. We believe the best thing a married couple can do for their kids, extended family, and the world is to build a strong marriage.

Life & Leadership Lesson: If you're married or plan to marry, this relationship is central to your life. Next to your walk with God, it is most important. Goodness radiates from your marriage relationship into the lives of your children, parents, siblings, colleagues, and friends. If you build a strong marriage, it will overflow into the rest of your life.

"You made all the delicate,
inner parts of my body and knit me
together in my mother's womb. You
watched me as I was being formed
in utter seclusion, as I was woven
together in the dark of the womb.
You saw me before I was born."

—Psalm 139:13,15-16a, NLT

Life Is Significant

My life's work is all about people even though I can barely call myself an extrovert. I'm fascinated about people because each one is a unique creation. Everyone of us is birthed into a state of dependence and we grow to a place of independence only to learn that we should live in a space of inter-dependence with one another. To do so, we must see ourselves and one another as God sees us.

ALICIA

She seemed to come out of nowhere. She walked in unannounced but impossible to miss. She was striking. Blond, petite, and beautiful. Her personality was pleasant and she carried herself with grace. Her presence was angelic. She was only fifteen. I don't know how she heard about our youth gatherings but Alicia made an immediate and positive impression.

We were organizing a trip to Mexico. Our mission was to visit and serve an orphanage full of children. She wanted to go. She insisted. We politely explained that there were no more vacancies. She was determined. She had a strength about her that was extremely unusual. Against my better judgment, I made a way and she became part of the group.

We did not have any problems with Alicia while on the trip. She was easy to get along with and seemed to mix in without a problem. One would think she was a long-time core member. Once we arrived, she shined even more. She had a way with these kids like I had never seen. Her Spanish seemed fluid. That shocked me since you would have never guessed by her outward appearance. She never used her bilingual gift as qualifying leverage. She became our super star within hours.

She seemed too good to be true. But I was smiling inside and out, looking forward to seeing what God had in store for this young talent. As we began to make our way home, the trip was considered a huge success. We arrived safely and everyone went back to their routines.

A few weeks passed and Alicia had not been back to even one of our regular gatherings. I began to look into her odd disappearance and learned from one of our students that she was heading to the hospital for a procedure. I gathered the details and a few hours later was at her bedside. She told me she was having a cyst removed and everything would be fine. I prayed with her and left her in good hands.

I never saw Alicia again. I learned later that she did not have a cyst. She lied. She had an abortion.

No matter how hard I tried, I could not reach her. I could not find her. She left us like she appeared. Out of nowhere. I can't imagine what was going through her mind the day she knew she was pregnant. The bus ride to Mexico. Loving on the children. The bus ride home. The decision. The act.

I don't know any more details. I don't know who else was involved. I don't know what kind of guidance or support she had. I don't know where she is today. I pray she is safe. I pray she has found God's unconditional love. I pray she has experienced healing. I pray that I will see her again. In this life or the next. She is important to God and to those who know her, regardless.

At the top of this chapter, we looked at the proclamation of God's intentional and loving creation of every living soul. The words are poetic and powerful. They should cause a pause for each of us. God knows us. We are not an accident. In the next chapter, I want to consider just a few ideas that add substance and purpose to our existence beyond our miraculous birth.

Life & Leadership Lesson: I had no idea the battle that was going on inside of this young woman. That should be a lesson enough. Each of us should consider the ignorance we carry in regard to our fellow man. Maybe it would be wiser to assume each one we meet is in a battle. If we did, how might that make us better people and leaders?

"God has made us rich beyond our dreams in the opportunity to experience and participate in all He has done and continues to do."

—Jim Piper, Jr.

Life Has Purpose

One of the greatest stories yet to be told is the one you are creating. God's story is about creating room for yours. He is a giver, not a taker. You cannot outgive God. No matter your trials or difficulties, your life has meaning. It has purpose. It has life! Sometimes we forget and that's when we need to take a step back to remember.

Have you ever stood underneath a star-filled sky at night? It's an amazing experience. On one hand, you are struck by the vastness of creation. On the other hand, it can make you feel small and insignificant. If you're a little bit philosophical, you realize something odd. You did not choose to be here. You did not choose to be born. Someone made that choice for you. And for those of us who belong to the vast majority, we are grateful. Once we did not exist but now we do.

Though life is not always what we wish it would be, it's an amazing gift and opportunity. So, who gave us life and why? Are we simply the glory of a man and woman who came together with the intention of conceiving a child? Was our conception an accident, a surprise, or the result of something that should've never happened? Regardless of the details of human activity, ideal or otherwise, God made you!

God did not make a sea of humanity in one great and massive creation storm. He creates one person at a time. That makes you extremely significant. Once you get captivated by God's intention, His decision to create you, a natural and new question arrives, why? Why did God create you? What is His purpose? The answers to these questions will align your heart and mind to your Creator, providing direction, meaning, and energy to your life. The answers are found through observation as well as from the testimony of Scripture.

FATHER

To begin, start seeing God as your heavenly Father. Do not allow the weaknesses or the absence of an earthly father filter, blind, or block you from embracing this truth. If it does, this may be your first obstacle to overcome. As you begin to personalize your faith in God, seeing Him as your heavenly Father, you will see your personhood take shape and it will fuel the rest of your life.

RELATIONSHIPS

Many years ago, I was attending a Zig Ziglar conference in Denver, Colorado. Zig suggested we all do something to increase our level of gratitude. He called it "The Wall of Gratitude." He instructed us to think about the most significant relationships in our history. People who have helped us, mentored us, inspired us, corrected us, etc. He told us to write these names on a document and frame it. He told us to think about each one and why they made my Wall of Gratitude.

This was our assigned exercise and I enthusiastically embraced it. In fact, I could not contain my excitement to work on it later. I had to start right away. So, I left the main arena, found a chair in the hallway and started my work. It was easy. Many people have made my life better but it was not difficult to identify the Hall of Fame in my life.

Let me mention something I discovered along the way. Many of the names I have included on my Wall of Gratitude is what you might expect. Family members, teachers, coaches, faithful friends from childhood or early adulthood, staff members, unusual clients, donors, a boss here and there. That kind of thing. And I have a lot to be grateful for! In addition, God brings people in your life when you least expect it.

Rhonda and I met Brian and his bride, Rosalie, now dear friends, on the patio of an Italian restaurant in southern California. What was meant to be a simple brunch through mutual friends, turned into lunch, dinner, and a whole lot of conversation. We connected. Today, he serves on my board of directors and is one of those guys who brings joy to my soul. He makes me laugh. I've never seen him uptight or hard to get along with. He leans in when he thinks he should. He does things right. He's down to earth. I just love the guy! Do you have a friend like that?

We share many common interests and concerns. And most of all, we are brothers in the faith.

Your life is full of relational opportunities.

STEWARDSHIP

You have the DNA for imagination, creativity, management, courage, and problem solving. You are a steward of your slice of creation. According to a casual perusal of the dictionary, DNA is considered the fundamental and distinctive characteristics or qualities of someone or something, especially when regarded as unchangeable. In other words, DNA is the raw material God gathers from a man and woman to create another human being. Biblically speaking, DNA is SUPERNATURAL dirt. It's the uniquely chosen dirt God used when He breathed life into you just as He did when He formed Adam and gave him life. The creation account says, *Then the Lord God formed the man from the dust of the ground. He breathed the breath of life into the man's nostrils, and the man became a living person.*[3] The distinction of human DNA is another clue revealing God's purposes.

Again, in the Genesis account, we find God apparently in conversation with Himself or what we will later learn through the testimony of the Scriptures, a conversation within the community of the Triune God: Father, Son, and Holy Spirit. Within this

[3] Genesis 2:7, NLT

conversation we see the intent to frame our DNA in His image. *Then God said, "Let us make human beings in our image, to be like us. **They will reign…** " [over all other creatures on earth]. So God created human beings in his own image. In the image of God he created them; male and female he created them.* [4] Part of our DNA is to rule like He does. Not to His capacity or His vastness; nonetheless, the ability and natural desire to steward creation is purposed in us.

Stewardship begins by taking inventory of what God has already entrusted to you. Your strengths, experiences, relationships, and opportunities are given to you for a purpose. Too many people are distracted by what others have instead of paying attention to what they've been given to develop. It's a universal problem. Appreciate and make the most of what you have. If you do that, most likely, you will see it grow. Focus on what you have, not on what you don't. Invest what you have and watch it grow. Just as a well-groomed person, a home and garden well maintained, a job well done, is noticed by many, so will your stewardship be recognized and rewarded. This too is God's design.

LANDSCAPE

God planted Adam and Eve inside a garden surrounded by wilderness. He empowered them to expand, to grow, to subdue. To literally landscape

---

[4] Genesis 1:26a, 27, emphasis in brackets is mine

the earth with people and beauty. In other words, His desire to express Himself through creation has been transmitted to you. You were designed to bring beauty to the world.

God is still in partnership with humanity in the creation of things. He partners with parents to create new and unique individuals. And everyone He creates has the opportunity to make their mark on the world, to the parent's delight and to the glory of God. When you give your talents to inspire or help others, God is revealing Himself through you. God doesn't need us, but He chooses to include us. He has given you the opportunity of life. You can squander it in foolish living or you can invest it in God's long-term plans. What you do today has the ability to live beyond you and into eternity.

John Maxwell recently wrote these words, "How you view things is how you will do things." I believe this is true. If you see little purpose in your life, you will think surviving is success. What a shame. If you see your family as an opportunity to demonstrate love and appreciation, you will see the good, and you will honor them. If you see your workplace as an opportunity to learn, grow, and contribute, you will be promoted. If you see your neighborhood as a place to build relationships, you will find ways to serve and be viewed as a community leader. If you see your life as an opportunity to add value to God's creation, you will become an ambassador of Heaven. If you see wrongs that must be corrected, and do something about it, you will be rewarded where it matters most. Outside of time and into eternity.

GOD

"It's not about you." Those are the first four words in Rick Warren's bestselling book, *The Purpose Driven Life*, of which, over 50 million copies in more than 135 languages have been sold. The marquee statement, "It's not about you," is as counter-cultural as it gets in a world consumed by self. A life centered on self is full of pressure and anxiety. It's like a body of water that only receives and does not overflow. It becomes stagnant, stank, and poisonous. Why? Because you were not created to serve yourself. Life is not about you, it's about God.

Let me say it another way. What you're looking for won't come from you, it will come from the One who created you. Did you feel the weight come off your shoulders? You should feel lighter just thinking about it. It should cause you to reframe your thinking from trying to be in charge and in control of your life to knowing that God is in charge and in control of your life, if you'll let Him. It's like having a "Get Out of Jail Free" card. You're able to walk out of the prison of your past and your worries for today and tomorrow. If God is in charge of your life, He determines and directs your purpose. Warren describes what he means by "It's not about you" with the following explanation.

The purpose of your life is far greater than your own personal fulfillment, your peace of mind, or even your happiness. It's far greater than your family, your career, or even your wildest dreams and ambitions. If you want to know why you were placed on this planet, you must begin with God. You were born by his purpose and for his purpose.[5]

I understood intellectually what Rick was saying, yet his words were so powerfully written, they stopped me in my tracks like a refreshing breeze on a hot summer day. What I realized was that all of these "good" things in my life were driving me. And all of them were crying for my attention. I was running from one to the other. They were defining me. I was out of alignment with God because I was not allowing Him to direct His purposes in and through me. I was a slave to so many masters!

The weight and pressure of trying to serve all these internal and external voices were lifted when I realized the best life is a God-centered, God-directed life. It's a life that is conscious of God's presence and delight. That sounds mysterious doesn't it? Is there a voice from heaven to guide your day? Is there an internal GPS providing direction? How do you discern your thoughts from God's thoughts? What if you make a

---

[5] *The Purpose Driven Life*, page 17

mistake? What if you pray and see no obvious results? What does it mean to be made for God and directed by Him? All good questions.

YOU ARE HERE

Remember those amusement park maps on display? They have a star or some sort of graphic that says, YOU ARE HERE. It's your point of reference so you can figure out which direction to go. Just like the sign, to live with purpose you must start here: TRUST.

Living out God's purpose in your life requires trust. You have to intentionally place Him at the center of your life just as intentionally as God decided to create you. One of the most memorized sections of Scripture is Proverbs 3:5-6:

> Trust in the Lord with all your heart; do not depend on your own understanding. Seek his will in all you do, and he will show you which path to take.[6]

To trust God with all your heart means to trust Him above all other concerns and desires. You trust Him eternally, not just for today. You will be disappointed from time to time while journeying through your life. Your desires will not always be fulfilled yet

---

[6] New Living Translation

you stand firm in your conviction that God makes all things right in His time.

Your understanding will fail you. It is nearsighted and limited. You must place your trust in God's character above your limited perspectives. As you seek Him for direction, comfort, healing, perspective, wisdom, and strength, do not be surprised to find out that His ways are not yours.

I remember the faith-filled words Norman Vincent Peale penned, memorized, and spoke often during his life, *"God is with me, God is helping me, God is guiding me."* This is where you should begin. Memorize this phrase. Speak it aloud as you continue down the path of purpose. As you do, your hunger for Scripture will increase. Your longing for prayer will come. Your convictions will rise. Your inner strength will grow. You will realize it is God who has made you more significant than you once thought.

Life & Leadership Lesson: The best way to live this life is to align yourself with God by embracing the concept of being made in His image and likeness. As an image bearer, you will see the world differently. You will see yourself as not only a recipient of the redemptive story but also a proactive distributor of grace. This is why the behavior of praying, *"God, you are with me, you are helping me, and you are guiding me,"* begins to align your attitudes and behaviors into a positive and redemptive force.

"Guard your heart above all else,
for it determines the course
of your life."

—Proverbs 4:23, NLT

Work on Your Life

The world is filled with too many people low on passion and purpose. Too many victims, too many looking for handouts. Too many working for the weekend. Too many living off of sugar!

I LOVE SUGAR

While visiting my son and his family in Germany where he was serving in the Air Force, my three-year-old grandson approached me, "Papa, sugar is bad for us." I agreed with him while we stood pondering what might come next. Then, with clear conviction, he said, "I love sugar," and walked away. It's true, isn't it? We know something is bad for us, but we do it anyway.

Have you ever asked, "How did I get myself into this mess?" Or maybe, "Why did I do that?" Or "Why did I say that?" Or "Why did I agree to that?" You probably have because it bothers you when you become your own worst enemy. Maybe you feel surrounded by your circumstances like a hiker lost in the woods with no apparent way out. Perhaps it's your job. Your financial situation. Your relationships. Your health. Maybe you struggle with your emotions: anger, anxiety, insecurity, jealousy, disappointment, or various levels of depression.

Maybe you're a high energy get-it-done kind of person but feel like you're running from one thing to the next and not sure why. If you resonate with one or more of these symptoms, welcome to the human race. Perhaps that's why we sometimes call it the rat race. Hurrying and scurrying while passing a mass of humanity wherever we go. Get in your car or catch a ride to the airport while trying to beat the traffic. Get on a plane to the next city and you experience the same thing. Cars everywhere, traffic jams, people looking past one another on their way to somewhere for something. It's a rat race indeed.

I've heard several business consultants and speakers tell working professionals and entrepreneurs, "Work on your business, not just in it." This is a common and conceptual phrase shared inside many business circles, especially in the realm of entrepreneurship because the task usually requires a broad scope of activities and skill sets. It's the "work smart not just hard" idea. The concept of "working on" promotes thoughtfulness, strategy, and wisdom. Working on is contrasted to working in. Working on means to step outside of the details, demands, and duties, so that you can examine the business as a physician examines a patient. The examination considers symptoms while looking for root causes. These findings allow the doctor to prescribe a corrective course of action. Working in the business is to follow the course of action.

It might surprise you that many business consultants encourage leaders to set aside as much as fifty percent of their time "working on" their endeavors. This percentage obviously moves up and down based upon the needs of the business, the season, and the level of one's leadership. The point remains. Successful leaders invest significant time working on their key relationships, evaluating the organization's performance, planning, and strategizing.

I wasn't exposed to this terminology until well after college. Though my classes described many facets of business, leadership is a concept academic institutions fail at miserably no matter what they title their curriculum. The concept of working on versus working in came while I was beginning my career as a business banker and especially as I became an avid reader.

To emphasize this point, I gathered a small collection of popular quotes you've probably read or heard before:

"Don't just work hard, work smart. The goal is not to work for money, but to have money work for you." —Robert Kiyosaki

"If you don't design your own life plan, chances are you'll fall into someone else's plan. And guess what they have planned for you? Not much." —Jim Rohn

"It's not the daily increase but daily decrease. Hack away at the unessential."   —Bruce Lee

"The most important investment you can make is in yourself."   —Warren Buffett

"The ultimate goal is not to be successful in business, but to have a successful life."
—Zig Ziglar

"If you don't make the time to work on creating the life you want, you're eventually going to be forced to spend a lot of time dealing with a life you don't want."   —Kevin Ngo

"The only true security in life comes from knowing that every single day you are improving yourself in some way."   —Tony Robbins

"Your time is limited, don't waste it living someone else's life."   —Steve Jobs

"Seek first the Kingdom of God above all else, and live righteously, and he will give you everything you need."   —Jesus

This concept applies just as well to our personal lives as it does our professional lives. In fact, I suggest it is more important to your personal life than your professional life because it's you that fuels what you do. You are the golden goose. You are the secret sauce. You are the one that works in and on your life and business. That tells me something very important. After everything is said and done, you are the business. I'll say it again, you are your business.

PAINFUL SYMPTOMS

When you live your life without working on it, it's like going out to sea without a map, a compass, or an experienced sailor to navigate the nuances of the ocean's currents, elements, and storms. What would that be like? Would you be capsized by a tempest? Crash into the rocks? End up in enemy territory? Die due to thirst, starvation, or disease? Maybe you'd be one of the fortunate ones rescued with an opportunity to start again but this time with the right planning, tools, and people to help you.

Millions of people live without giving much thought to the importance of their daily lives and how the days compound into significant positive or negative results over time. Consider some of the most common symptoms of a life drifting at sea, going through the motions, just trying to cope and get by:

- *Being a Passenger*
  You are sitting on someone else's bus. You don't know where you are going and you don't know why. You blame your situation

on The Man, the company, the economy, the government. You're a pawn on someone's chessboard.

- *Weight Gain & Poor Health*
  Most weight gain and physical health challenges sneak up on us like an unsuspected mugger. It feels like it came upon you suddenly when in most cases, it took years to take hold.

- *Broken & Strained Relationships*
  It wasn't a big fight or a big mistake. It was a series of neglects both small and large that led to the fight. It was a series of smaller missteps that led to the big mistake. It was neglect, one day at a time.

- *Addictions*
  It started off as a small pleasure, a lapse of judgment. But then it turned into a regular vice and then an addiction. Now, it's a real problem. Once it was not in your life, but now it is the battle of your life.

- *Money Problems*
  Why is it that money problems find their way into the lives of the rich and famous as well as the young couple just starting

out and everyone in between? Is it just bad luck? A bad bet? Hard times? Or is it something else?

- *Poor Job Performance*
Your boss doesn't like you. In fact, many of your previous bosses didn't like you. Your coworkers don't have your back. You don't like your job. It must be the system. Everyone expects too much. Your view of work is that it is a necessary evil instead of an opportunity to add value. When did you acquire this perspective? Where did it come from?

- *Small Faith & Little Hope*
Perhaps the most concerning symptom of all. Your worldview is not appealing but you have almost accepted it as fate. The agnostic and atheistic ideas of some have tempted you to take a look inside their world. In a weird way, it has become your ally against the disappointments and perceived betrayals of your childhood faith. It didn't happen all at once but year by year you've confused faith. You failed to recognize that your faith is only as good as the object of your faith. Your faith fails you when it's placed in the wrong things.

These examples are all around us. You don't wish them upon others and you certainly don't want them hanging around your neck! If you struggle with one or more of these or something not listed, you can indeed reverse the symptoms by dealing with the root problems.

ROOT PROBLEM

"There are a thousand hacking at the branches of evil to one who is striking at the root."

—Henry David Thoreau.

I appreciate this quote because it reminds me of the gap between activity and thoughtful activity. Both the thousand hacking at the branches and the one striking at the root, mean well. They are fighting the same enemy. They are teammates but one is much more effective than the other. The difference is in the approach. One recognizes the symptoms and attacks right away. I can't judge him too harshly because at least he is in the battle! The other is much more effective. The one striking at the root invested the time to consider the source and then attacked there.

Thoreau's statement identifies both the root problem itself and the typical ineffective method for solving the problem. The problem in our lives, our person, our relationships, and our work, is evil. Evil has a very extensive wardrobe. If I were to attempt to list how evil dresses itself up, I could easily fill several pages. For now, let's consider a few examples: evil dresses itself up as selfishness, covetousness, laziness, lying, cheating, short-cuts, cowardness. You know the drill. It also accessorizes its wardrobe with insecurity, insincerity, bribery, and flattery. Evil perverts. It counterfeits. It teaches you from the lofty university of lies. You are taught to believe things about you, the people in your life, and your work that mislead and corrupt what is potentially good.

The root problem, therefore, is two sides of the same coin. One side is evil and the other side is how evil has trained you to cope, to numb the symptoms just like cold and flu medicine helps us get through those dreary days of cold and fever. It actually works for a little while but think about what life would be like if you lived on cold medicine every day. Think about that.

THE PRESCRIPTION

Work on your life. There is an effective antidote to the presence and work of evil in your life.

I will ask you to exercise your mind by stepping outside of yourself, your relationships, and your work and examine yourself from that vantage point. This ability to think about our lives, to work on our lives, is what separates us from the animal kingdom. We have the God-given ability to think about our origin, our direction, and our destiny. By doing so, we will intentionally construct a true and healthy worldview.

Your worldview is the lens you look through to see the world. You interpret and interact with the world through your belief system while moving toward and fulfilling your purpose. You align and shape your worldview by intentionally moving from concepts to attitudes and from attitudes to behaviors. Your life will naturally overflow into the lives of others, spilling into opportunities for relationship and leadership.

You will have to shape your worldview while navigating in and through a world that is divided, scattered, confused, and noisy. As you succeed aligning concepts to attitudes and then attitudes to behaviors, you will be offering new perspectives, faith, discipline, purpose, and a sound mind to the world around you. The world will still be broken but you will have the strength to embrace that fact because you will also see God's redeeming work constantly on display.

Life & Leadership Lesson: We become better people and we practice better leadership when we align ourselves to God's desire for us. We do that by intentionally working on our lives—our concepts, attitudes, and behaviors. To start, we must believe there is good and evil; more importantly, we must believe there is hope because there is God.

PART III

LEADERSHIP STORIES
THAT SHAPE US

"The most dangerous leadership myth is that leaders are born—that there is a genetic factor to leadership. This myth asserts that people simply either have certain charismatic qualities or not. That's nonsense; in fact, the opposite is true. Leaders are made rather than born."

—Warren Bennis

" ————————————

"Nothing grabs my attention
more than watching a young
person strive to be excellent, to
work extremely hard, and separate
himself or herself from the norm."

—Jim Piper, Jr.

———————————— **"**

Empowering Others

To be employed at Jensen's you had to stand out. You were required to wear a clean and pressed white dress shirt and necktie. Hair had to be off the collar and ears. There was a minimum walking speed limit. It needed to look like you were hustling without being frantic or bumping into customers.

These expectations were explained during the interview process. I didn't think one way or another about them because I was excited to start my first real job. These were the conditions of employment, plain and simple. It was 1975, I was fifteen-and-a-half years old and my starting wage was $2.10 an hour.

Mike Kelly was my boss. He was reasonable and clear while providing consistent feedback whether positive or corrective. Mr. Kelly was a professional and easy to respect. During the first month or so, he kept me busy around the dairy section. Though it seemed like I was completing an array of tasks, he was actually training me, step by step and day by day.

I learned terms like "perishable foods" and "expiration dates". I was introduced to words, ideas, and skills that had to do with reducing spoils, stocking, reducing overstock, rotating stock, facing off rows, taking inventory, pricing, newspaper ads, non-toxic cleaning, suppliers, and ordering. I was being introduced to a whole new world and I loved it.

YOU OWN IT

After a relatively short time of training, Mr. Kelly brought me out in front of the dairy section. He examined it with an expression of appreciation. Where he looked, I looked. Then he looked at me with a purposeful pause. I'll never forget what happened next.

During that look, Mr. Kelly said, "Jimmy, this is yours. You are in charge of the dairy. You own it. It's your business and I know you will make us proud." Those may not have been the exact words but that's how I remember it. And with it came a pay raise. I think it was 25 cents, making my new wage $2.35 an hour. I was in the money!

Thinking back on those days, I decided to "Google" Jensen's. I was pleasantly surprised to learn about its expansion of stores, a continual commitment to quality, and an elevated grocery and bakery experience. I also found the following statement:

> Gene Fulton began his career at Jensen's in 1957 as a clean up boy at age 17. He worked his way up to the position of general manager, and in 1970 made arrangements with Mr. Jensen whereby he would purchase Jensen's upon Mr. Jensen's retirement on January 1, 1981.

Mr. Fulton's story, in part, describes the culture of the organization. He was the GM when I was put in charge of his dairy. I'm confident it would have been probable for me to still be there if that were my desire. We were encouraged to think of ourselves as owners. It was and perhaps still is a place of opportunity. It was the Jensen way.

The culture of responsibility, professionalism, and reward was thick. For the ambitious person, Jensen's was a gold mine of learning, confidence building, and advancement. It was a place where I was allowed to take on new and expanded territory far beyond my age or experience. That's why I loved it. It was both exciting and challenging.

High performers and leaders don't hang around where there is little challenge or opportunity. It wasn't easy getting up at 4 in the morning to drive into work before school started. I was there for the purpose of stripping off the old wax floors and replacing them with that glossy shine and intoxicating aroma of new wax.

There were three incentives for being the floor man. First, you got the opportunity to operate the miniature Zamboni-like floor machine. That honor was entrusted to a select few.

Second, you became friends with the bakers! The only way into the building at that time in the morning was through the back door of the bakery. Wow! That was my response to the smell of the freshly baked bread and pastries. The bakers couldn't help it when they saw this poor high school kid shuffling his feet along the flour-dusted floors while wiping sleepers from his eyes. They knew my favorite treat and they would have it waiting for me. A freshly baked strawberry-filled glazed donut! I loved those guys and ate more than my share of donuts!

Third, Jensen's didn't trust the scheduled stripping and waxing to just anybody. They paid $5 an hour. That was good money for a teenaged employee. I gladly learned, ate my donut, and did those floors with excellence. Then I would run off to school and come right back to work after my last class or if it was wrestling season, after practice. It would make for a long day.

I was eventually wooed away to a competitor with what turned out to be empty promises and a completely different experience in every way imaginable. However, I learned that not all grocery stores are created equal just like any grouping. You will attract the best talent by differentiating yourself from the average, the boring, and the disappointing. You can become Jensen's-like if you set your standards high without apology.

Life & Leadership Lesson: I didn't know it at the time but Jensen's and high school wrestling prepared me for life. They taught me about hard work. It's more important than raw talent. They taught me about ownership. Ownership is when we take responsibility for something. They taught me about respect. When you respect yourself, you offer respect to others, and in return, you often receive respect from others. Empowering others starts by striving to create excellence because it attracts those who desire the same. *And it is sustained when you provide a piece of the pie to those who will "own" the whole pie with you.*

> "No one should despise your youth... be an example... in speech, in conduct, in love, in faith, in purity."
>
> —The Apostle Paul

Goodbye Insecurity!

When you're young and healthy, it's impossible to fully appreciate because you have no personal experience with being old or weak. If you're young and ambitious, you take exception to people who look down on you because you're young. When I was young, I never thought much about my age until someone reminded me. I was too busy pursuing goals and new adventures.

One of my team members approached my desk, informing me about a customer's demand to speak to the manager. I walked toward the person he pointed out. She was probably in her fifties and did not look happy. As I extended my hand, her facial expression painted a portrait of disbelief. Her countenance transitioned from irritation to offense and shock. She took a half step back, stood up straight as if we were about to begin a fencing duel, and said, "You cannot be the manager!"

GROW A MUSTACHE

Indeed I was. Thanks to the management training program, it accelerated my career far beyond my peers. I was twenty-five years old, Manager and Assistant Vice-President of a bank in one of the wealthiest areas of southern California. Being of Celtic descent, ruddy in complexion, my peach fuzz mustache did not help matters. I looked like a seventeen-year-old boy trying to impress school girls.

I wasn't insulted by the jab. Actually, I'm sure I was but not fully aware of it at the moment. It's game time. No time to become offended. After a while, one learns to emotionally dodge low blows and insults. By now, I was conditioned to deal with insensitive, adolescent, and condescending comments. I suppose these kinds of situations oddly reminded me of personal achievements while at the same time, deafening my ears to the jeers from spectators peering into my arena.

One of my favorite things about God is how He examines us. He does not look at the obvious things—appearance, stature, age, or even our mistakes. He looks deeper. When the prophet Samuel was considering the next King of Israel, God instructed him with these words:

> "Do not look at his appearance or his stature, because I have rejected him. Man does not see what the Lord sees, for man sees what is visible, but the Lord sees the heart." —I Samuel 16:7

The playgrounds of life choose leaders based upon the outer appearance. God and one's destiny has a much different playbook.

Knowing God sees into my heart humbles me because He knows me better than anyone. I cannot hide from Him. He knows my fears, failures, and secrets. That might seem like bad news but it's not. It's good news for at least two reasons: He loves me in spite of it and while I cannot change much of my outward appearance, with God's help, I can change my inner person.

It was my boss's idea for me to grow a mustache. He saw what we all saw and was trying to help. Weeks later, when he came to visit and beheld the outcome of his advice, he encouraged me to shave it off. The experiment was officially classified a failure.

Over the course of years, learning leaders feel more at home in their own skin. They don't need to rely on fancy titles, expensive clothes, cars, houses, and such. They don't need to be concerned about their age, gender, or height. Obviously, professionalism and a pleasant appearance is vital for every leader but they need to take stock of what is really important. And they probably don't need to grow a mustache but their inner child needs to grow up and never stop learning.

Learning and growing is important for all of us but it is essential for leaders. During one of my podcast interviews with Johnny Sirpilla, the bestselling author of *Life is Hard but I'll Be OK*, the topic of insecurity came up in our discussion. Johnny asserted that all workplace conflicts are rooted in insecurity. If that's true, even if it's most often true, it behooves us to look deep inside ourselves to increase our self-awareness. Where else can personal transformation begin?

If you think a little about the flashback moment between me and the bank customer, there was plenty of insecurity floating around. My peach fuzz mustache was an attempt to disguise my youth. My customer's frustration with the bank made her feel like a victim and my presence as a potential solution might have been another blow against her need for validation. Sending a boy to do a man's job is insulting, don't you know? Insecurity and competition filled the air before an understandable word could be spoken.

My training kicked in. My customer's issues were not about me. It was about the problem and her anxiety attached to the moment. I needed to demonstrate respect and strength by focussing on the issue, not the emotions. Easier said than done, but on this day, I was successful. It was an easy fix and just about any one of my fifty team members could have helped her but she didn't know that and she was too riled up to consider the possibility.

This was my first encounter with her but not my last. Over the next eighteen months, we chatted on several occasions. I learned more about her as a person. I learned more about her history. I learned that everyone has a story and every story includes hardships. The small box of Christmas cookies she left on my desk was a wonderful reminder of how important it is to push insecurities out of our lives, relationships, and leadership.

Life & Leadership Lesson: Insecurity is part of our lives and leadership. The sooner we acknowledge them and seek to understand them, the sooner we will grow. As we drag them into the light, we will no longer be mastered by them. Insecurities may desire to be passengers in your car but better they be in the back seat rather than behind the wheel.

"The ultimate measure of a man is
not where he stands in moments
of comfort and convenience,
but where he stands at times of
challenge and controversy."

—Martin Luther King Jr.

You and Your Boss

I have come to believe one of the main differences between one leader and another is not just their innate styles but the amount of pressure they are able to hold. It's similar to the air compressor sitting in my garage. If I leave it on for too long, the relief valve is triggered and the compressed air roars out of the canister. How much pressure can you hold? Do you know how to relieve it in a healthy and consistent way?

MR. PILLAR

There is no doubt in my mind, God brought us together because we needed each other. Steve Pillar was a retired marine and now a Vice-President at Bank of America. Every weekday without fail, you could find him at his desk reading the Wall Street Journal while sipping his coffee, well before the crack of dawn. His white dress shirt always starched, tie carefully knotted, and shoes polished.

I was in my early twenties and always a southern California shorts and T-shirt kind of guy. I was learning how to look the part. Like most young men, arriving at the office by eight o'clock was a feat in and of itself. "Good afternoon" was the phrase I'd often hear at 7:45 AM as I walked toward the adjacent desk. Just another day with Mr. Pillar.

His standards were high and his vocabulary was stuck in time back at the marine barracks, I think. "He's a tough man to work for," I would hear as I was navigating through my young career. "Most don't make it a year working for that guy," I heard more than a dozen times during my first twelve months. He was tough, that's for sure.

Excuses were not tolerated, ever. Our face-to-face encounters were sometimes as close as six inches. At times, I was beginning to believe that I enlisted in the Marines instead of the banking sector. More than once, I found myself taking a personal break inside one of the men's restroom stalls wiping tears away while trying to get a grip on myself. It's embarrassing to admit but nonetheless true.

Some people struggle finding the correlation between work and faith. Even as a young paperboy, I would ride my bike delivering early in the morning before light. I remember praying on many occasions for God's protection. My years at the bank were no exception. While sitting in the stall, I would pray. I'd ask God for strength. I'd ask for wisdom. Once my emotions were back in check, I would get up and get back at it.

I'm sure it helped to pray but things really changed once my prayers changed. Instead of praying for me, I began to pray for Steve. This change of heart and direction happened as a result of learning more about him and a verse I came across during my daily Scripture readings.

I had learned about some of Steve's past experiences in life through a colleague. Tragic kinds of things. I became more empathetic toward him and less threatened. It always helps our relationships when we know more about one another. I also ran across a verse in the Old Testament book of Job, chapter forty-two and verse ten.

After Job had prayed for his friends, the Lord restored his prosperity and doubled his previous possessions.

I certainly could not compare my frustrations with my boss to the trials, tribulations, and tragedies of Job, but God used the verse to change my perspective.

Make no mistake, I still needed strength and wisdom. And that's exactly what God provided through more background on my boss and spiritual direction from the Scriptures. The intersection of Scripture and new information became a defining moment. Mr. Pillar was not my enemy, he was my employer. He was my friend. Even though his tactics were not always appreciated, he wanted me to succeed.

Once I got that straight in my head, I became his advocate. I worked my tail off. When he said jump, I would ask, "How high?" When he was unreasonable, I would stand my ground by offering respectful alternatives even if we were six inches apart. We became a team. He didn't know what happened but I did.

He got his money's worth in laughs when he invited me to the country club for golf. There he was sporting his fancy attire along with another associate and a customer. Then there was me. I had never played golf before so I ran out to K-mart and found some white golf shoes. I thought the tee holders sewed onto the right side of each shoe was a handy idea. That's until the guys fell over in laughter revealing my purchase of ladies golf shoes. That was embarrassing!

First, it was golf, then tennis. We even enjoyed some dirt bike rides into the hills near his home. On occasion, he would invite me to his place to see some of his woodworking projects. His shop was something to behold. Large machines, hand-held power tools, paints, varnishes, and racks of wood waiting to be turned into furniture.

Steve graduated from boss to mentor. I graduated from moralist to openly honest and loyal employee. Together, we became a team. He taught me about banking but he taught me more about leadership.

While sitting in his car, parked in the most distant space from the bank building, he would teach me. He pointed out the three flag poles and which of the three flags, American, State of California, and Bank of America should be placed where and why. He taught me to notice the condition of the parking lot, the landscaping, the building itself, and the windows. He taught me to see everything.

Then came the promotions, one after the other, until he turned the keys over to me. I didn't see him as often anymore. We worked out of different offices from that point on. He was still my supervisor and the guy I would call in a pinch. Along the journey, I became known more for being the guy who survived Mr. Pillar than any other title the bank gave me.

The day came for me to say goodbye. It was one of the hardest things I've ever done. One of my mentors told me I would be stupid to move on from the bank. My father told me to follow what I believed God was leading me to do. My pastor warned me that what I was about to step into was probably not everything I thought it would be.

I was surprised that Steve was not surprised. He asked me a few clarifying questions but accepted my resignation. As we gathered my staff one morning before opening the doors for customers, Steve stood up in front of the crowd announcing my soon-to-be departure. He explained with tears in his eyes that I would be leaving to serve the Man upstairs.

Life & Leadership Lesson: Don't run from tough situations. If you walk through them, they will teach you more than you can imagine. They will also provide strength and wisdom for the days ahead. When you look back, you'll see it as training. You'll probably see it as child's play too because you have grown and have the capacity to handle much more. What once felt unbearable, feels almost normal.

> "We are what we repeatedly do.
> Excellence, then, is not an act
> but a habit."
>
> —Will Durant

Go Upstream

A couple of years before leaving the bank and diving headlong into ministry, I was having lunch with Gary. He was my pastor at the time. We were at McDonald's just down the street from my office. I don't remember exactly what we were talking about but it was intense and it was about faith. It was one of those conversations where you could lose yourself unaware of your surroundings as well as the time.

I was startled by the sudden vibration of my pager. Pagers, sometimes called beepers, came before the mobile phone. They had a few settings: audible alert sound, vibrate, or silent. They were small electronic devices with a tiny window display typically fastened to a person's belt or thrown in a purse if fashion was a concern. I looked down at the message recognizing it was code for "We need you back at the bank ASAP!" In one fluid motion, I began walking back to the office while saying goodbye for now. Though I was heading in the direction of the bank, my mind was still captivated by our God-talk.

She must have seen me coming because the door opened right in front of me as if our team just completed a fresh set of hospitality training. "They are in the conference room waiting for you", she said. "Who are THEY?" I replied with some confusion in my voice. While trying to catch up to my rapid pace, she told me it was about a delinquent commercial loan and a weird cease-and-desist letter.

As I entered the room, several of my team members were there with bewildered looks on their faces. As they described the situation, it was easy to see we had made a clerical error recording a deed of trust as collateral for a loan now delinquent. The cease-and-desist letter came from the attorney of another property owner demanding we stop harassing them with threats of foreclosure.

We had secured the business loan with the wrong property address. I don't need to go into any more detail than that. However, my sharp MBA graduate who had made the loan was hiding his face in his hands. The Escrow officer in charge of accurate documentation had red blotches spreading all over her neck and face. The others in attendance were either there to support their comrades or saw an opportunity to have front row seats to a disaster. Of which I'm not certain.

IN THE ZONE

It took about five minutes for me to see with my own eyes what had happened and what our exposure might be. Still securely planted in my God-thoughts stemming from the last ninety minutes at McDonald's, I fluidly moved into the next obvious step. I quickly confessed to the team that I did not know what to do but pray. I bowed my head and began to pray aloud.

It took me about three sentences to realize what I was doing. I was praying publicly in the bank conference room about an asset dilemma. What in the world was I thinking?

I pumped the brakes on my flow of words in order to navigate the speed bump ahead while realizing I was living in two parallel worlds—the world of prayer and the world of material things. I opened my eyes to peek at the reaction from the room. To my shock and disbelief, every single person had their head bowed and were seemingly agreeing with me in prayer! With restored but humble confidence, I finished the prayer and acted like this was a normal thing... not the loan issue, the prayer thing... at work.

I never heard a negative comment from that event. I also don't remember the outcome of the issue. It must have corrected itself, otherwise I would be able to recall something that significant. You might be thinking you could never do anything like lead a group of people in prayer at work. Neither did I, but remember, it was not a conscious act. I think there is something to learn here.

Faith is not a private matter. What is going on inside of us cannot be contained within our personal structure. Like the pores of our skin, we let out energy. We radiate what is inside. It is dynamic in nature. It's much more than personality, it's about what we are connecting to and who we are connecting with. It's about paying attention to what we allow inside ourselves. Whatever we allow in will find its way out. If we heed this truth, it's really good news.

We become the kind of people we want to be by intentionally choosing our spiritual diet. McDonald's was probably not the best physical choice for us to make that day but the fellowship and the content was a game changer. It was so impactful, it stuck with me. I wish we could hear something or learn something in one sitting but that's not usually the case. We tend to be leaky buckets, so we need to be constantly filling ourselves with good stuff because we face challenges all day, every day.

Life & Leadership Lesson: Healthy people and leaders hike upstream to manage what flows downstream. To transform our thinking and behavior, we must concentrate on what is being poured into us. Many leaders simply try to manage what flows out. Everything leaks. You will either spill out good or foul. It all depends upon what you allow into your mind, spirit, and body.

"Boundary events vary from individual to individual, but in general, boundary events are change signals. They mark the end and then the beginning of a significant time in a leader's life."

—Dr. J. Robert Clinton,
The Making of a Leader

Going All In

The out-of-date phone in my office buzzed. I pressed the button labeled INT. I assumed it was the abbreviated version for intercom. Frona was on the other side of the phone and the other side of a thin piece of drywall that separated my office from her workspace. I could have heard her just as easily if she chose to speak through the wall instead of the phone. She said my mom was on line one.

MARCH 09, 1987

As soon as I heard Mom's voice, I cried. Why was I so emotional? No one died. No one was sick. I'm a grown man for God's sake! It should have been a day of levity. It was my birthday and it was the first day of a new chapter in my life.

On the other hand, I just walked away from a successful banking profession with nothing but promise for the future. It was a really good situation. At one point in my young journey, I had secret aspirations of becoming chairman of the board. The work was never boring and I was always learning. In my last role, I was a business banker while also opening new concepts of banking around the inland empire of southern California. It fit me like a hand in glove.

The contrast between then and the new reality had something to do with my emotions. The building I was now sitting in was a refurbished WWII army barracks, serving as both a church office and Sunday School space for children. My first steps into my new office revealed a very outdated shag-carpeted room with petrified boogers on the wall, one dated armchair, a phone book, and a prehistoric telephone sitting on top of the phone book which was sitting in the seat of the chair. Other than the office manager, no one was there to greet me. I had no idea what I was supposed to be doing.

The previous two weeks were filled with goodbye parties and well wishes. Everyone was very gracious. I was leaving a community where I was well-connected and involved. Our house was up for sale and we were moving closer to Los Angeles. We were moving to Chino, California, to serve as youth pastors.

Most people move for a promotion and a substantial raise in pay. Not in this case. My salary was being cut in half, my benefits almost completely gone, and the housing market was substantially more expensive. From a temporal perspective, not smart at all but this is what I wanted to do.

After I pulled myself together, Mom encouraged me to meditate on Psalm 46:10, which reads, "Be still and know that I am God." This verse teaches us that when we are anxious for whatever reason, it is good to stop. To stop striving, stop talking, and maybe stop thinking so much. Instead, remember that God is in control. He is not anxious. He knows me, cares about me, and that is enough.

The call helped me even though I was a little embarrassed and surprised by my emotions. Apparently, the call also changed the plans my folks had for the day. A few hours later, they pulled up to the church parking lot, walked inside, and announced we were all going for ice cream. I was touched by their intentional expression of love and support. I was still embarrassed and felt like a four-year-old kid wearing shorts, white socks up to my knees, and one of those hats with the little propeller on top.

Not everyone supported my decision to bow out of corporate America. Ken, one of my mentors from a local service club, expressed in no uncertain terms that I was making a big mistake. I will leave out his exact and colorful words in order to keep this book suitable for all readers. To make my point clear, he has never spoken to me again. He never returned one phone call. At some point, one moves on.

No doubt, my odds for accumulating greater wealth would have come by staying on the banking path and Lord knows we need good people swimming in the financial sectors. It's not like I did not know what I was leaving behind, but it just didn't matter anymore. When you are a person of faith, it has application. When God moves in your life, it cannot be denied. It really is that simple. I never saw it coming but when it did there was no turning back.

The house sold quickly and we found a place to rent. It was time to set up our new home which was walking distance from the church, create a strategy to reach and serve the youth of the Chino valley, and figure out how to make ends meet. It was game time and we stepped onto the court ready to give it all. We did not come to dip our toes in the water. We came to make a dent in the darkness.

Looking back, I should have worked harder at aligning the existing team to the new vision. I was turbo charged with passion while lacking the leadership experience working with volunteers. One thing is for sure, they all knew I meant business. Let's just say, I ruffled feathers and didn't even know until I heard from the grapevine.

We had Fridays off so I did some business and financial consulting on the side. We also started a small yard care company. We had some savings coming from the proceeds of selling our home in Hemet as well as cashing out our stock options from the bank. That's how we made ends meet for a couple of years until the growth of the ministry was able to meet our needs.

Fast forward six years from March 9, 1987, the youth ministry grew to reach hundreds of junior and senior high students and many of their families. The stories are both deep and wide. Some could even be called modern-day miracles. And though I had experienced blessed seasons in the past and even more later, this season just might be my favorite.

Life & Leadership Lesson: To accomplish something bigger than yourself, you must make an all-out commitment holding nothing back. Faith is not a theory. When God begins to move, He is turning your spiritual fat into muscle. He is preparing you for your next quest. Do not be afraid of what you do not know or cannot see. Believe that where He guides you, He will provide for you.

"Two are better than one, because
they have a good return for their
labor: If either of them falls down,
one can help the other up. But pity
anyone who falls and has no one
to help them up. Also, if two lie
down together, they will keep warm.
But how can one keep warm alone?
Though one may be overpowered,
two can defend themselves.
A cord of three strands is not
quickly broken."

—Ecclesiastes 4:9-12, NIV

Now That's a Partnership

Pastor Dan Vasquez was first my boss and then he became my pastor. From there we became fast friends and partners in ministry. Partnerships like ours are few and far between in this life. If you ever experience a life-giving partnership, you should consciously and gratefully acknowledge, nurture, and protect it. That's exactly what we did.

On the front end of our time together, I had nothing but youth ministry on my heart and mind. I was all about reaching kids—all of them if I could. My passion was fueled by first-hand experiences growing up and into my early to mid-twenties. I saw and felt things that rerouted my life and still affect me to this day. Many of my friends and circles of influence were void of a faith-centered life. I was struck by the contrast of what it means to live with faith or without it and was convinced I had taken mine for granted. I was dumbfounded by the realization that many in my own backyard were walking through life without a God consciousness.

I've seen what happens to youth who grow up within homes and micro-communities unaware of the nearness of God. Without the benefit of a well thought out faith to guide them, they are shaped into an object of one's culture while being courted by the media to believe and follow a variety of juicy propositions. But when youth are equipped with cerebral and spiritual skill sets, they are able to divide truth from error. Even better, they may sense a calling to become an ambassador to their generation thus slowing down the cancer that seeks to destroy the quest for God. The Christian faith is not soft and without logic as some might think. It is also not cruel and condemning. It is cerebral, spiritual, and full of goodness and hope. This prose was the foundation for my ministry mindset. The reason behind my passion and activity.

ALIGNED

Dan's mindset was similar. Ten years my senior, he was focussed on children. While I was going after the teens and twenties of our day, he was casting a vision to reach families with kids from birth through elementary school. This similarity of focus and shared faith in the God of the Bible provided a strong foundation on which to build a partnership. We built our relationship through mutual respect, appreciation of our individual skill sets, time together for prayer, play, and planning, and by including one another in our places of influence.

BACK-TO-BACK

Our partnership had another quality many don't realize. We watched the other's back. In this crazy world, there are three kinds of people in every organization.

The promoters, predictors, and punishers. Promoters are positive builders of the vision and mission. The predictors are the ones in the shadows waiting to say, "I told you so". The punishers are those who have been inflicted by their past and consciously or unconsciously work to destroy what others are trying to build. Take it or leave it but if your partnership does not include a spine of loyalty greater than the schemes of this world, it will fail.

I've also seen promoters descend into predictors and predictors into punishers. There are a variety of reasons why this happens but it's probably not too different from Judas' fall from grace as one of Jesus' inner circle to the betrayer. Once he realized the mission did not align with his own desires, the descent began. It started with objecting and then distancing. Then he graduated to resentment and betrayal. Punishers have a point to prove so they don't stop until it's too late. The name Judas will always be synonymous with betrayer.

People hear what they want to hear and believe what they want to believe because they join teams with unexamined motives. Those who are self-aware know this so they work hard for months to align themselves to the mission and vision of their new team and organization. They realize they have joined something that has already been established so their role is to enhance not to challenge. Their role is to serve the mission, not to create their own. Both Dan and I learned this the hard way but our saving grace was found in our partnership. We stood back-to-back.

We did not see fruit from our plans and labors as fast as we wanted. This caused frustration for us. Sometimes we would blame ourselves. Sometimes the congregation. Sometimes God. This is what humans do regardless of their titles.

THE SUMMIT

On one rainy day it all came to a head. The two of us were sitting in his white Datsun B210. The windows inside the car were fogging up as our conference room on wheels hosted our summit. We were exhausted, emotionally and spiritually. We cared for one another but something had to change. It was one of those days when friendship and partnership is tested. In different ways, we both decided to quit.

That lasted for less than five minutes. After I left his car, I walked into the office to grab a few things before heading home. As I reentered the parking lot toward my car, he was waiting and motioned me to approach. He had rolled the window down to speak while a tear began trailing down his left cheek. He was recanting his decision to throw in the towel. While I was standing in a light sprinkle, he reminded me (and certainly himself) that while he was a UPS driver, he prayed ten years for the opportunity to pastor a church. To quit now would be wrong. He was determined to get back in the fight—emotionally and spiritually. He apologized for some of the things he said earlier while supporting whatever I decided to do.

Sherri Coale, a hall of fame college basketball coach writes in her book, *Rooted to Rise*, "*Life gives you no guarantees. But I know one thing: if you sell out and lose, it will mean more to you than if you go through the motions and win. It's not about what you get at the end. It's about how you choose to live the pursuit.*" I didn't have her book or her statement in those days but her sentiment is almost exactly what I was feeling.

I chose to stay. Dan demonstrated several core strengths as our first chair leader. He was consistent, prepared, and dedicated. He was a pious man. I saw him as clean inside and out. His leadership provided the foundation for mine. I was a risk-taking, outreaching, take-the-hill kind of a leader. I was creative and he was empowering. He was six-foot-something and I was five foot six on a good day. He was a high school track star and I was a high school wrestling champion. When we played one-on-one basketball, it brought the best out of us. We would laugh and argue. When the game was over, we looked like we had been in a street fight.

The church started growing rapidly. The youth ministry had outgrown the seating capacity of our facilities and we became one of the largest and fastest growing youth ministries in the region, if not beyond. Lives were being changed and all of a sudden, our peers saw us as experts but we knew the truth. **No human is an expert in ministry.**

What changed? How did exponential growth happen when before there was little to speak of all while doing the same things? The conferences, the planning, the changes, the execution, these were all well established and should have brought results long before the summit. The change happened at the summit. It's only natural to expect what you expect but what happens when the result is disappointing?

Here was the change. Before, we unknowingly were working for a result or an outcome. What we were doing was right and good but it was leveraged by the weight of outcomes. Dan's come-to-Jesus meeting led us back to doing what we were doing because it was right and good and that would be enough. The rest was out of our hands. I don't know what else to say on this matter.

Our partnership continued to grow wider and deeper. It became more mature than ever. We created a plan of expansion that few know about even to this day. It was an exciting plan like none I had ever seen or heard before. It was unique because it rose out of the DNA of our partnership and the young leadership rising from our faith community.

We were in the process of rebranding our ministry to The People Place. Momentum and optimism filled the air. Plenty of people were noticing and joining the movement. That's good and bad. It's difficult to know why someone jumps on your bandwagon, especially when things are going well. Motives can be very illusive and sometimes hiding in the shadows. Dan was discerning and thoughtful, so he was able to regulate the speed of our leadership-onboarding process. Almost everything was positive and moving forward until our world lost one of the great ones.

July 9, 1993, Dan passed from this life. He was forty-three years old and in the prime of his life. He left behind his bride, three children, and a thriving ministry. Over the previous nine months, he was literally doing everything he could to beat cancer, but it was not to be. His memorial service was one of the largest I have ever attended. I used his well-worn Bible to speak from at the service. Between the church gathering and the graveside, the event lasted all day.

The baton was passed to me but I had lost my partner and had no desire or leading from God to take his place. The leaders rallied around me and we strategized. These faithful souls thought they knew the vision but they didn't. Much of it was still baking in the oven and the baker was gone. There was no doubt in my mind, the uniqueness of our vision and strategy required both of us. I could not sit in his chair any more than he could have sat in mine. That's what made us a team. It was time to charter a new course.

Charter a new course we did. We added new leaders and congregations to the movement. We acquired assets and a vision for the future. The church would retain its legal name, Chino Valley Community Church, and eventually the baton was handed to a new leader well suited for the days ahead. Today, the beautiful campus sits in Chino Hills, California, and has become a beacon of light to the community.

Life & Leadership Lesson: Life-giving partnerships are not easy to find because they are built from the ground up. The mistake many make is where they place their focus: on the product, the business, the outcome. For a partnership to work and thrive, the primary focus must be on the partnership itself. When you do that, you have the strength to weather storms, achieve amazing things, and when it ends you cherish it all.

"Tell me and I forget,
teach me and I may remember,
involve me and I learn."

—Benjamin Franklin

No Perfect Report Card
for Leaders

Scripture sets the table for what many Christians call Holy Communion, the sacred practice of remembering what Jesus Christ did on our behalf, with these words: "Examine yourselves..." (1 Corinthians 11:28, NRSV).

The command is powerful because it makes plain the importance of self-examination. Our lives count. We are not perfect but we should be learning and growing. We should not take our days for granted. That's why I named our podcast about life and leadership, The Today Counts Show.

TWELVE AND A HALF YEARS

I learned more about myself, humanity, and leadership during a twelve-and-a-half-year run while planting churches in Denver, Colorado, than at any other stretch in my life. To be clear, the learning was not simply a result of activity, it was the result of purposeful activity, the willingness to get out of my comfort zone, and the discipline of self-examination. In reflection, I did some things right due to thoughtful preparation and specific training as well as from past experiences from my days as a young banking executive and then as a pastor. But hold on, I also made plenty of new mistakes as a result of naivety, character flaws, and lack of self-awareness.

I could easily dedicate an entire book to this decade-plus timeframe but for now, I'll use the following two chapters to squeeze out the juicy stuff, the best from both sides of the ledger. Afterall, hindsight is 20/20. If that's true, let's look back and benefit from it. My journal entries from those days provide more wisdom for today than they did then because now I'm able to observe from a higher elevation. I am now separated from the day-to-day chaos, adrenaline rushes, and emotions of that day.

Through the discipline of reflection, I'm able to articulate convictions and newly discovered lessons galvanizing them into principles. I write them. Writing requires careful thought and increases the odds of personal transformation. Some of the principles I will share with you were formed over many years prior to this season of ministry while others introduced themselves in a not-so-pleasant manner. I learned them the hard way. Painful yet useful for growing to those who choose to be teachable. Not everyone who grows old grows wise.

I consider each principle a golden nugget, valuable in its own right. And as I recognize and gather them one by one, they are like a bag of gold, a fortune of wisdom and strength.

Reflection must be done at a higher elevation, so that you can broaden and deepen your perspective. A zoom lens allows you to bring distant objects into focus. Helpful for a close-up view but not as helpful gaining context. A wide-angle lens provides a broader picture providing context. Both lenses are needed. Attempting to reflect while surrounded by the tall buildings, noise, and pollution of your daily life will prove ineffective. When you're in your situation, you cannot see the bigger picture without getting to higher ground. A panorama perspective improves your ability to navigate the day-to-day in a more-informed manner.

You must pull away from time to time to learn, grow, and gain a healthy mindset. Change cannot occur until you change your mind. Think of the times you were sitting in the window seat as your flight began its descent toward the runway. As you look down upon the city, all seems peaceful. Everything appears to be in order. There is no litter, graffiti, honking horns, arguments, or illnesses. Just peace and order. From that elevation you can see the city structure. You recognize certain landmarks and because you have visited some of those locations, you are able to recall certain details and memories attached to that place. Now you're able to see it from a distance and up close.

Above the fray is a good place to be as you consider both the beauty and the realities of life and leadership. There is order and there is peace but it is not found by accident. The big picture provides an advantage as you consider how to re-enter your reality. It will increase your ability to be calm under pressure, present instead of scattered, and empathetic instead of impatient.

Some enter every day with little thought. They get up and do what they do. Eventually, this way of living loses meaning and purpose. Some try to forget the shadows of their past as if it has no value whatsoever. They cut it off to protect themselves from the emotions and memories. This robs them of deep waters of understanding and wisdom. Some try to change the true narrative by replacing it with make believe. This choice is living a lie.

Life & Leadership Lesson: Life is filled with wins and losses. Both are rich in content for learning and growing. Embrace your wins. Celebrate them. Study them. Embrace your losses. Study them. Integrate them into your life's story and watch how the two transform you into an authentic person and leader.

"The secret to success is
to do the common things
uncommonly well."

—John D. Rockefeller

Five Fundamentals

During the twelve-and-a-half-year run, I practiced three of five fundamentals well, and two, not so well. These fundamentals apply to us all in any season of life but especially when starting something new or entering a new season.

IT'S A THREE-LEGGED RACE

This is a lesson we learned almost a decade prior. A pastor and mentor once told me that I could run only as fast and far as my bride was willing to go. We were partners in a three-legged race. We literally had to learn how to run together.

His advice was given in the context of ministry but I find it holistically true. At the very least, married couples need to be connected and supportive in their individual endeavors.

I know too many ministry couples who are not in it together. Let me be clear, if you're not aligned at home, the cracks in your foundation will spread to the rest of what you are trying to build. Your profession, your ministry, your dreams must be built on a foundation of unity.

For us, we have always added value to what we were doing in our individual ways but we were partners from beginning to end as we are today. Just like in a three-legged race, you have to wait for the other to place their leg into the potato sack. Then you have to walk to get your timing right. Then you run. If one falls, you wait, you walk, you run.

FINANCIAL STRESS WILL SINK YOUR SHIP

When we started the journey to Colorado, I was only thirty-five years old. I had plenty of energy and was in good health. We did not have much materially speaking, but we did have a decent revenue stream and we had no debt of any kind other than the debt to love God and others.

I see too many folks trying to start something new while weighed down in debt. You simply cannot sustain fighting two battles at the same time. Your new adventure is the battle. This principle gave us the freedom and the strength to fight one battle. When you can leverage all you are and all you have in one battle, your odds of winning increase dramatically.

GET A COACH

We were trained for church planting by some of the best and experienced leaders from the International School of Theology in Arrowhead Springs, CA. The training included all of the pragmatics and logical steps of church planting. We were also coached to watch out for typical hazards, obstacles, speed bumps, and potholes along the way. These included certain kinds of people, governmental regulations, cultural opposition, and a variety of nuances related to starting something new.

We were provided with a Church Planter's Toolkit. The kit's process mirrored the birth cycle—conception, prenatal, birth, growth. Each of these stages of development included key milestones and tasks to be completed before moving to the next phase. It was a proven process that we followed to the letter. I still remember one of the key phrases that caught my attention. 87 percent of mistakes in the life cycle of a new organization happen during the conception phase!

To this day, I caution leaders to take their time working through the conception phase! When you include others, the process cultivates ownership, organization, and momentum.

GOTTA BE SELF-AWARE

Accomplishments teach you about your strengths but they hide your weaknesses. Beware of success too soon. It is a liar.

If there is a golden nugget larger than the others, self-awareness might be it. It's a buzz word today but nonetheless important. It is required for sustaining health and competent leadership. It is a prerequisite to emotional intelligence and appropriate behavior. If we are unable to lead ourselves in a healthy and moral manner, how can we lead others in the same way? To be self aware requires humility, reflection, strong and capable coaching, and a willingness to be held accountable.

We could have done better in this area.

BEGIN WITH THE END IN MIND

Keeping the end in mind is one of Stephen Covey's *Seven Habits of Highly Effective People*. Keeping the end in mind was a big fail for me. My vision went out ten years but it was accomplished in less than five. By the time year seven and eight came around, I was lost. I had no plan beyond that. I think it caught me by surprise.

I flew to Chicago to meet with Mike Andres, the President of McDonald's USA. As I walked into his office, which once belonged to Ray Kroc, I was admiring McDonald's history on display. Mike added to the history lesson by telling me that washing Mr. Kroc's private plane was his first job as a young man and Mike's father was Mr. Kroc's personal pilot.

We shared a laugh or two about this story. While grinning, Mike said, "My first job as a teenager at McDonald's was washing the company plane. My last job, I got to ride in the back." Pretty cool story.

During my visit, I learned a valuable lesson from Mike. While we discussed his transformational vision for the then troubled corporation, he knew what it would look like when he was finished. While he identified with the company at a personal level, he was also able to differentiate his value as a person from his lofty role as the corporate leader. He was already forming thoughts about what was next after he accomplished his goals at McDonald's.

Until then, I never realized the power of Covey's Second Habit. You can't keep the end in mind if you never visualized it from the beginning. Seeing the end of your tenure from the beginning helps you better prepare for it in every way. It helps you see yourself as a steward of the opportunity instead of your identity.

Life & Leadership Lessons: As you reflect, learn, and grow, establish your leadership fundamentals. Teach them to others. Leadership lessons should not be private. Your lessons should benefit not only you but those around you.

"

> "The best way to predict the future
> is to create it."
>
> —Peter Drucker

"

Sustaining Next-Level Leadership

When you invest over a decade of your life into one thing, you learn what is fundamental to success and you learn what sustains it. I have come to find the practices and mindsets sustaining high performance are far more valuable than the ones that provide a momentary taste or experience of success. The two are different. And the practices that sustain success are not recognized by the masses.

The overriding mindset that sustains high performers is gratitude and service. Leading is an opportunity to serve. Some call it a burden. I suppose both are true. High performance, moral and effective leadership, does require more. Yet the truth remains, gratitude for life and the opportunity to make things better is a sustaining power.

There are more staples to sustaining success. The following were difficult for me to learn but they taught me that leadership was higher than my natural strengths or the things I was good at or the things I like doing. Leadership was, in fact, doing what needs to be done. Sustaining leadership is next-level leadership.

DILIGENT COMMUNICATION

Scripture says: "Do you see those who are skillful in their work? They will serve kings; they will not serve common people" (Proverbs 22:29, NRSV).

Skill comes only through the grind of diligence. Nothing can replace diligence. It is an aspect of noble character. Even the most gifted of people will not achieve their highest potential without it. It is the positive side of stubbornness. It is a persistent focus on getting better and doing things right. Some people and teams win simply because they don't quit. They wear out their opponents or the obstacles in their way.

Several months after landing my first "real job" as a banking executive, my boss asked me a question. "Do you know why I hired you?" As I looked up with a puzzled expression, he continued. "I hired you because you wouldn't go away. You just kept showing up!" It's true. I did. I wouldn't leave the guy alone until he said yes. I knew it was an opportunity of a lifetime and I was going to wrestle the situation until the final whistle blew.

Becoming a skillful leader is no exception. It requires a "no quit" attitude which is not easily translated when leading others. My attitude as a younger leader looked a lot like this: "If I said it once, I said it. Why would I need to say it again? If I have to constantly remind and follow up, isn't something wrong with you? Am I a micromanager? Are my team members incapable? Do they just forget? Are they being passive-aggressive?

What the heck!? It's exhausting!" These are natural feelings but they must be tempered with diligence.

If you're going to be effective as a leader, communication is a constant. If leadership is anything, it is diligence. Vision leaks. Just like your body burns calories and disperses water, vision leaks out of organizations. You have to fill your body every day with healthy calories and plenty of water. If you want to be an effective leader, you cannot grow weary filling your organization with vision. You may feel like you are nagging or speaking down to people. Resist this feeling and keep explaining the why and how for what you do and what you are all about.

DEFINE EXCELLENCE

Do less but do it really well. Almost everyone who is serious about creating or providing something worth consuming believes in excellence. The weakness of such philosophy is that excellence is rarely defined. When does something become excellent? When is it good enough? When is trying to do more a waste of resources with a diminishing return on *energy* and investment?

A quest for excellence is not always well received because it is not clearly understood. With limited resources, you want to invest in the most important things. In general, you should refuse to start something or add something if you cannot define and sustain excellence. Doing a few things very well means you have to choose not to do other things. When you are stubborn about this, you'll profit. When you give in, it will hurt you.

CREATE CULTURE

Galvanize culture through routine. I've heard it said that culture happens by default or by design. I believe this is true. Some think the right culture is simply a reflection of themselves. If you want a culture that mimics you, then all you have to do is be you and the culture will follow your lead. If you have enough self-awareness and humility, that should scare you to death because you know your individual attitudes and behaviors fall short of a broader and winning culture. It takes a team!

The DNA of a winning culture requires much more than the calling and personality of the leader. It requires a team, a community, an army galvanized through time and routine. Hold consistent activities that align values, beliefs, and practices toward the accomplishment of the vision. Bring individuals into a unifying team-building process that demonstrates what winning looks like.

Galvanizing culture and values through routine requires short-term sacrifices by every individual in order to create long-term gains—an authentic community committed to the chief aim. These short-term sacrifices, not overbearing, not exhausting, but well thought out and executed, compound over a period of time into a sense of belonging, loyalty, and ownership.

Nothing builds culture better than investing time together planning, defining, practicing, correcting, losing, repairing, winning, and celebrating. As your culture becomes more defined, it is able to provide an additional layer of protection for the organization. It recognizes and removes imposters, waste, and poor performance. If you are looking for a sustaining supplement to your leadership, galvanize your desired culture through routine.

CHARACTER VS TALENT

Choosing Talent over... I made the mistake more than once by allowing talent to persuade me. Talent is one of those shiny things that grabs your attention. It represents the short-cut, the quick fix, the deep breath of satisfaction. Then talent steps aside and you meet the real person hiding in the shadows. It's not talent's fault, it's mine.

Most of my poor decisions came when I was tired. Not physically, but emotionally. Usually during those times you feel like you are losing momentum. That's when you start grasping at straws instead of backing up and gaining perspective before re-entering the arena.

I recall one of my leadership contexts where two teams overlapped and collided. The first team was not trained or experienced in ministry. Most of them were volunteers or paid small stipends. They came into their roles by way of relationship, friendship, and a shared past of some kind. I knew them and they knew me. The relational and historical connection cultivated loyalty to one another while also honoring the mission at hand. This proved to lay the foundation for strong character and hard work. Don't miss this... teams become a force of character more powerful than any one individual, no matter how talented.

The second team came later. They were well-paid, experienced, and loaded with talent for the context. In the beginning, we were amazed and they brought about a sense of freshness and hope to a tired but faithful group. Some came through our internal systems offering promises too good to be true and they were. Most came from outside of us. Almost as passersby. There was no relationship, no history, no regard for our story, no reverence for what was at stake.

Put those two teams together and you have a train-wreck. Yep, that's what I did. I tried to marry these two teams. They divorced and it was ugly.

As a friend and advisor to leaders, those who work with me today know how long and hard I preach team alignment. The wounds of this mistake run deep. You need talent but not at the expense of alignment. Never.

KNOW WHAT YOU CANNOT DELEGATE

Delegation frees up leaders to do what needs to be done in their organizations. It's a vital skill set that grows an organization and sustains leadership. Those who cannot delegate will never elevate their leadership to a place where they have an accurate pulse and perspective of their organization.

There are some things you just cannot delegate. You can't delegate your opinion of a team member within your reach. You cannot delegate vision. You cannot delegate culture. You cannot delegate the ultimate responsibility of the actions and performance of the organization. You can share all of these but you cannot delegate them. Finally, you cannot delegate values.

Values are the boundaries of decision-making. They are the guardrails protecting travelers on the road to your vision. I'll say it again, you cannot delegate values. You've read about values before but I've dedicated the next chapter to the subject of values because of my deeply held convictions that they are a difference maker.

I have delegated some of these responsibilities in my past and have suffered for it. When you truly care about something, decision-making is difficult. When you don't really care, you make decisions of convenience. That's the difference. As the leader and the number-one believer, you have to stand up for these and never trust them to a hireling. Sounds harsh, I know.

NEVER STOP LEARNING

Forsake the Lone Ranger Bravado. You never have to be a lone ranger. On the front end of my first season of trailblazing, I was a dedicated learner soaking up wisdom from anyone who had gone before me into the wild wild west of church planting. Looking back, it made a very positive difference. I felt confident and supported.

As the road continued, sometimes the advice all sounded the same or simply did not apply. As you slowly begin to bow out of the coaching groups, conferences, and mentoring relationships, something sneaky begins to happen. You lose touch with the outside world. The objective world. The world where you can find relationships, support, and stories that gird up your strength and wisdom. If you are not careful, your success will fool you into believing that you are the exception to the rule. You are not.

Life & Leadership Lesson: There are attitudes and practices that cultivate leadership momentum and outcomes. There are leadership attitudes and practices that cultivate and sustain leadership health. It's important to consider the difference between the two and practice both. This is the challenge of giving your life in service to others.

"The highest caliber of leaders consistently demonstrates a commitment to values even when no one is around. This is called integrity."

—Erin Porteous

Putting in the Work

I met Erin through another client who has become a dear friend. She is one of those "all-in" leaders. She is altruistic, relational, and a goal-oriented achiever. We put in a lot of time discussing culture and the importance of dynamic values. As she put in the work to articulate her values, I found them to be simple, easy to understand, and attractive. I thought they would be useful for not only her continued success as an individual but also in shaping her leadership team and then the culture of her organization.

TOO MANY EQUALS NONE

Much like goal setting, we almost immediately agreed that too many stated values are as good as none. Too many goals are as good as none. Research has bore this out. We simply do not have the capacity to hear the voice of too many shepherds. We do not have the energy, resources, and focus to chase too many goals. We end up accomplishing none.

It's not that we do not appreciate dozens of values. It's not that we don't want to conquer dozens of goals. It's simply not effective. Effectiveness comes with focus. We have to make hard decisions to get the most power out of our energy and work. It's better to say, if nothing else gets done, this is what we will accomplish.

It's better to say, if we stand for anything, we stand for this.

ERIN PORTEOUS

Erin is the CEO of The Boys & Girls Clubs of Metro-Denver. I have enjoyed working with her over the past few years. I asked her to share her closely held values—the lenses she looks through while evaluating her leadership as well as shaping the culture of her team and organization. I believe her work below is worth the read.

FOUR VALUES

As leaders, we all have core values that we live by. Intentional leaders align both personal and professional values to make a succinct focus for anchoring priorities and ensuring consistency across all facets of their lives. The highest caliber of leaders consistently demonstrates a commitment to values even when no one is around. This is called integrity. And the interesting part is these micro-actions aren't grandiose in nature but rather small responses every single day through practice, consistency, and habit.

Here are a few simple examples of values practiced with integrity:

- Putting the shopping cart in the corral at night in the parking lot when no one is around even though it's faster to just leave the cart right at the front of your car (it won't move right?!)

- Restocking the toilet paper at work.
- Fixing the printer that you jammed even though no one knows you did it.

Most often when you find a leader who values hard work at their job you also see it in their home life. Odds are, hard work is what got them to a position of leadership. Or for another example, if someone believes in nurturing and growing others, they may ignite passion in work colleagues *and* tend to exhibit a strong EQ and commitment to the relationships in their personal lives.

Those who truly have defined and refined their values don't opt in and out depending on the setting, but rather, identify a set of principles and values to live by and then anchor themselves to those defining truths in all aspects of their lives.

As I approach the mature phase of my professional career, I can now reflect on my values and how they came to be over the years. We spend a good portion of our early years *learning* our values. Oftentimes, we can't even articulate that we are doing so, but our brain is constantly taking in information and then determining if it aligns with our constructs of how we believe the world works, or if it doesn't we pitch it. As we mature in our careers, we start to take the lessons we've learned, the philosophies we have seen, and frankly our observations of our bosses and colleagues to solidify what we like and don't like. From my career, one of the elements that have shaped my beliefs and style is seeing what I *don't want to be like* in how a boss treats me or others. If you are going through that now, don't discount the lessons you can learn through this experience. Sometimes it's easier to identify what we don't believe in, than what we do (Especially when we are young!).

My four core values for my professional and personal life have remained the same without much deviation through the decades; Hard work, Humility, Honesty, and Humor.

The difference is, in my younger years I was just *living* the values—and they launched me to the point I am at in my career today. But I wasn't in a place where I could talk about what they were and how they defined me.

Today, I can articulate my values and share them with others. These four values guide me as a believer in God, a spouse, a mother, a daughter, a sister, the current chairman of a prominent business group, and the CEO of a $20 million company with more than 250 employees. The point being, you won't see me act upon these in *some* roles in my life, while being dormant in others. My commitment to my values shines through all of the faucets, and one of the hardest is probably parenthood—the forever humbling role where I think I'm teaching my kids, but really they are instructing me on all the true things in life that matter most. So, let's define what these values mean to me.

Hard Work: I've held a lot of jobs through the years. It started with babysitting in middle school, then I moved into working in the hospitality field much of high school, college, and my twenties to supplement my nonprofit wages which weren't enough to pay all my bills. One of my jobs was working with food vendors at large concert festivals. I recall one night when the musicians had gone back to their hotels, concert goers had fled for their cars, and I was standing in a small refrigerated cooler truck counting tortillas so we could run our end of show inventory and reconcile the night. My fingers were so cold they were shaking and I kept losing count around 150 tortillas—which mattered since we charged by the unused product. There wasn't anything cool about my job, it was in fact kind of miserable. But it was in that moment of hard work that I figured out two things: I didn't want a job like that forever and I would work even harder to ensure that wasn't my fate, and, doing that kind of hard manual work, taught me to persevere. To stick with the hard stuff even when I really didn't want to. Back to my earlier point, leadership isn't one thing, it's a repetition of actions over and over, at an office, in relationships, and even when no one is looking and no one will know many hundreds of tortillas are left… except me.

Humility: When my brother and I were growing up, my dad was insistent that we say "I was wrong" when we were… well… wrong. As a kid, it was kind of an annoyance, but as an adult it's been fundamental in my willingness and ability to own my own actions. Whether it's with my husband, my kids, or a work colleague, when I goof up I'm able to "own it", so we can call it out and move on. The action of saying, "I'm sorry I was wrong," gives us the ability to swallow our pride (a hard thing to do), especially when many parts of society tell us that self-worth comes from building ourselves up. Humility is one of those simple but hard values to live by.

Honesty: There are two parts of honesty. The first is honesty to *self*. If we first and foremost are not honest with ourselves, we will never venture out of a stage of self-awareness to drive change and action. The second part of honesty is how we converse with others. As leaders, where the commitment to honesty can have the most impactful value is through courageous conversations with those we care about. It's that little Jiminy Cricket telling you, "You need to approach that difficult topic… You need to state your feelings about that issue that keeps reoccurring and why it's bothersome." It's easier to avoid the most important part of the conversation, honesty pushes us into a space of being authentic, transparent, and courageous.

Humor: This category has been present through my work for more than fifteen years working for a kid organization. We can never take ourselves too seriously, because humor is a great equalizer and one of the moments when we can be reminded of the joyful parts of life. Kids remind us of that every day. One of the successful components of humor is that it is usually most effective in the present tense. Yes, we can recall a past event that was funny or plan something that we think will make someone giggle in the future, but belly rolling and laughing out loud often happens when we are present in the situation. And that reminds us to be present, in all situations, giving our all, not our half, while the other part of our brain is on our smartphone, surfing the web or lost in our own thoughts.

Life & Leadership Lesson: Putting in the work to really think about—to discover your values. This alone differentiates one culture from another. The strengths of Erin's value set is that they are easy to remember. They are everyday words we are familiar with and her definitions are almost not needed. Some try to get too fancy and miss the boat here. Do you know what your closely held values are? Does your team? How do you use them to shape your culture?

"

We probably don't fight our Goliaths
the same way."

—Jim Piper, Jr.

"

Fight Like David

I've already established that I once wrestled and was pretty good at it. I also told you that wrestling taught me about discipline and hard work. What I didn't tell you is what it also did beyond that. It might be a boyish thing to say, but it's significant in a man's world. Wrestling taught me how to defend myself. On more than one occasion, wrestling proved itself more useful than being bigger or stronger. I never looked for a fight but for some reason, there are those who like to fight shorter men. I would not do well in boxing, but as soon as I got the big fella on the ground it was all over.

We live in a world of engineering, systems, manufacturing, and best practices. While all of these have their place and add value to our lives and leadership, there is nothing as remarkable as a man or woman called by God to fight a battle. To fight and win as they were designed by their Artist-Creator.

I enjoy the experience of walking into a new and elevated restaurant, a unique winery, an off-the-beaten-path place of business, a new custom home, and a magnificent cathedral, castle, or palace. It's in these places where you sense pride of ownership, creativity, and uniqueness. You can almost see the fingerprints and sense the soul of the person behind it all.

Contrast unique architectural designs of custom-built homes with track housing. One is expensive and grand, the other, inexpensive, common, and unimpressive. They both provide shelter but one inspires while the other does the minimum. Like me, you're an original, you are like a custom home.

Leaders are like custom homes. We find commonalities in both. Most houses have foundations, walls, roofs. Leaders have temperaments, strengths, and history. I suppose the world would be more interesting if every house was custom built but they're not. Leaders on the other hand, are uniquely shaped. Each and every one of them.

FIGHT LIKE DAVID

You might recall the story of David and Goliath. Knowing David was preparing for battle against Goliath, King Saul tries to clothe David in his tailored and kingly armor. To which David replies, "I cannot go with these, for I have not tested them." David then takes off King Saul's armor and goes to battle swift of foot and with marksmanship abilities like few others. With his slingshot, he knocks Goliath unconscious and then finishes him off with the giant's own sword.

This is a dramatic and inspiring example of authentic leadership. Authentic leadership is attractive.

Many of us have grown weary of the franchising experience where the owner's presence is absent. Where the original sense of ownership no longer exists. Where there is little ownership, there is disappointment. Authentic leadership is the principle of ownership. While universities work diligently to bottle the secrets of leadership as if it could be ingested like a super food or protein shake, God continues to create unique and authentic leaders to fight giants.

SPEAK IN YOUR OWN VOICE

This idea of authenticity reminds me of a time when Rhonda and I went to a week-long family camp together. While the kids were enjoying their programs, we were sitting in a hall listening to some of the best speakers in the world. I remember gently nudging my wife during one of the lectures and whispering to her, "When I grow up, I want to speak like him!" After a donut-and-coffee break, we were back at it listening to the next speaker. Once again, I leaned over and whispered, "The last guy was good but when I grow up, I want to speak like this guy!"

They were both amazing and effective communicators. One was not better than the other. They were different but they were both amazing. They were authentic.

If you try to organize authenticity out of a leader, you destroy what God is creating. Why would we want every church, ministry, and business to look and feel the same? Crazy. As my dad often says, "God starts doing something special and then we organize the special right out of it, we kill it." Of course, we need to be organized, but the authentic leader needs the support of a matching structure. Structure serves the mission. The mission does not serve the structure.

I recognized something powerful while reflecting upon the twelve-and-a-half-year season of planting churches. When I am healthy in heart, which is to say, mentally, emotionally, spiritually, and physically, I lead well. I lead strong. I lead wise. Perhaps this is true for all of us.

When any aspect of my being was not in alignment with the whole, I wasn't quite myself. I could think too much, allowing fear of losing the approval of others to creep into my spirit. Or I would take things too personally and lose objectivity. And if one fears they have something to lose, they play safe. Leading safe is actually very dangerous. Safe knows nothing. It does nothing. It has no conviction. It leads from the middle. It's no man's land.

Here's the problem, when we are unhealthy or out of balance in some way, we lose authenticity. We lose David's clarity of thought, conviction, self-awareness, courage, decisiveness, and sense of justice. When we are unhealthy in one way or another or when we are trying to be someone we are not, we simply don't know how to walk in our authentic self. We don't know how to fight in that armor.

Sometimes I would rationalize thinking I was being a servant leader when in fact I was becoming a puppet. When you care too much about what people think, you lose your moral authority. You lose authenticity. You lose your secret sauce. You lose your ability to fight and win.

Life & Leadership Lesson: I will sum up with some quick bullet points for you to consider as you strive to walk in the path God has made for you.

- Leadership is about convictions. It's good to collaborate but you can't lead if you don't know what matters. If you don't know what's worth fighting for.
- Leadership understands the power of authenticity. You can't fight your giants in someone else's armor.
- Leadership shapes culture. It does not try to reflect it. In fact, it is almost always counter cultural.
- Leadership has enemies. Grow up fast on this one. I was naive. I'm a good man. Who would want to take me out? Your greatest threat will come from those closest to you. No exceptions. You'll have spears thrown at you from a distance but that's not where the lethal threats come.
- Leadership creates a clear vision in the midst of competing visions. As you succeed, it provides more opportunities for others. Many of these will be in direct competition to your original idea.

Authenticity is attacked from all sides. You can learn and you can grow but be sure to fight in the armor God gave you.

Final Thoughts

First, thank you for giving me the opportunity and honor to speak into your life. Again, I encourage you to think about and embrace the fact that you are a unique creation of God. God's story includes you!

The people in your life are another opportunity you have to create stories that cannot be contained by this generation. They have the ability to be a blessing to a multitude of others whom you will never know, yet your fingerprints will be evident.

Your leadership is also a gift. See it as an opportunity to create stories of victories, comebacks, and even defeats for even they had value to our lives.

—Jim Piper, Jr.

www.ingramcontent.com/pod-product-compliance
Lightning Source LLC
Chambersburg PA
CBHW030504100426
42813CB00002B/325